A TIME TO GROW UP

A Daughter's Grief Memoir

LARADA HORNER-MILLER

Illustrated by
CHERYL HORNER-CHRISTENSEN

Horner Publishing Company

To buy books in quantity for corporate use or incentives, call **(505) 323-7098** or e-mail **larada@earthlink.net**

ISBN-13: 978-0996614429 (Horner Publishing Company)

ISBN-10:0996614427

�֎ Created with Vellum

CONTENTS

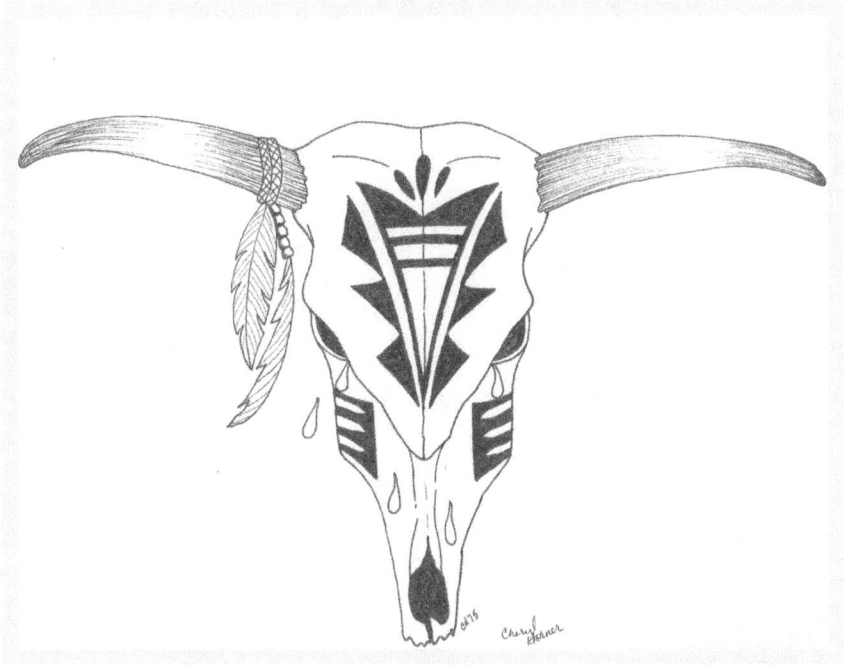

DEDICATION

I dedicate this book to my brother, Harold Horner (nicknamed "Bub"). He's walked beside me my whole life—through the good and the bad.

I would also like to dedicate this book to my loving husband, Lin Miller.

Both Bub and Lin were my rocks during my mom's sickness and through her death. I couldn't have survived without either of them.

Finally, I dedicate this book to my two nieces, Connie and Cheryl, and to my nephew, Andy. Love and support come in many shapes and actions, and they provided much of both throughout Mom's sickness and death.

ACKNOWLEDGMENTS

Susan Macnofsky, my therapist, listened to each one of my poems immediately after they were written. I cried as I read them to her, in the depth of my pain.

She said to me, "Please publish these poems as a book. I want my daughters to be able to read these poems after I pass."

Thank you, Susan, for your continued affirmation of me as a poet and writer.

And a big thank you to Jackie Ward for taking the picture for the cover of this book!

And to Cheryl Horner-Christensen for all of your precious drawings but especially the delightful angels.

"While I thought I was learning how to live, I have been learning how to die."

~Leonardo de Vinci

✻

Words spoken: "Each person grieves in his/her own way."
Actions done: Return to your normal life and live it!

~Elva Horner

✻

"We did not change as we grew older; we just became more clearly ourselves."

~Lynn Hall

PREFACE

The world fell apart when my dad died in 1996, but I stayed strong for my mom. It was when Mom died in 2013 that I completely crumbled. With both parents gone, I felt like an adult orphan.

Do you fear losing your parents? Have you lost one or both of your parents? It's been said, "When you lose your mother, you also lose your childhood." The loss of my parents altered my life.

How can I say I've grown up to be the woman I always wanted to be at sixty-three? Didn't I grow up to be an adult at eighteen? At twenty-one? At thirty-five?

My whole life I've looked at other women and judged their outer appearance and compared it to my inner landscape, and I always came up short—they were pretty, happy, and laughing. I wanted what they had. My inner life was chaotic—a war zone—and I had to keep up a false front to survive. I always came up less.

Prior to 1988, I never considered myself an alcoholic because I compared myself to my first husband. I knew he was one because he drank every day, drank a large amount, and became violent. But I was a binge drinker, and it took a while for me to realize it was also a problem because of this comparison. I could go a week or a month and not drink, but then when I did, I had no idea what might happen. Often the outcome was horrible.

In 1988, God intervened in my life, and I went into treatment for codependency. According to Mental Health America, codependency is "an emotional and behavioral condition that affects an individual's ability to have a healthy, satisfying relationship. It is also known as 'relationship addiction.'"[1]

At the codependency treatment center, we attended weekly AA (for alcoholics) and Al-Anon (for family members of alcoholics) meetings because then there were no CoDA (codependence anonymous) meetings in the area. I was at an AA meeting when I heard a woman tell her story, and it mirrored mine. That's when I knew I was an alcoholic. My life suddenly made sense after accepting that truth. I had thought I was crazy all those years; recovery was my answer.

I've been sober for twenty-eight years now. Both of my parents were alive when I got sober, and they supported me through the years.

During my life, I married four times. First, I was married to a raging alcoholic for eight years in my twenties; second, to a man in recovery for two years in my thirties; and third, in my forties, for twelve years—seven of which were in secret—to a man twenty-two years older than me.

My current marriage is the one I wanted my whole life! We knew each other for many years before we married, and we celebrated our fifth anniversary in 2016.

My recovery work has saved my life. I've stayed sober during many trials because I kept doing the program's suggestions: get a sponsor, attend meetings, and work the steps.

Because of my recovery and the growth I've made from it, I was emotionally present and sober for both of my parents' death—an amazing blessing for sure!

Over the years, I saw how Mom and Dad handled the loss of their parents. When my grandfather died, Dad cried with us at first but then he mourned in his solitary cowboy way—driving out to the ranch and going through his grief alone on the land he loved and had shared with his dad. When my grandmother died, again Dad privately grieved.

In the loss of Mom's parents, I saw her go through extreme mood swings. She cried with me and with others and showed her grief. Unlike Dad, she found comfort in grieving with others.

On January 6, 1996, my dad died. Losing my first parent left me reeling. This loss changed my life forever. At Dad's death, I was eight years sober. I had feared his death for years because of our close relationship. How could I survive without him, I wondered?

After losing him, I focused on Mom and her suffering. I did little in the way of thinking about processing my grief. Grief support groups didn't exist at this time. I continued my life as it was and made the best of it—my mom became my best teacher on how to handle grief.

I became Mom's primary caretaker—long distance from three hundred miles away and in a minimal way at first. More than anything, I supported her grief and business decisions concerning the ranch—I listened. We talked about Dad and how this big loss affected our every day lives. I enjoyed our close relationship and the time taken to acknowledge our grief.

She gave me, and many others, a timeless piece of advice, "Everyone mourns in his or her own way." I also saw her return to her normal routine and continuing living her rich, full life. Many well-meaning friends asked if Mom was going to move to Albuquerque to be near me, but I laughed. I knew she would live out her life in the community she loved, doing all the activities she loved. Some friends saw her as a weak woman who couldn't exist without Dad—she definitely proved them wrong.

Her process intrigued me because I resembled her more than Dad. She taught me how to grieve and it came in handy over the years that followed as my losses mounted with my age.

On March 23, 2013, Mom died, but this time was different and so very difficult. Both my parents were now gone and I felt alone, an "adult orphan." My recovery and faith in my Higher Power helped me survive losing her, but my main relief came through writing—I wrote poetry and lots of it. When I wrote a poem, tears of relief flooded me—a major healing tool. I read them to my therapist, and she cried with me. One particular night, she asked me to publish them so her daughters could read them after she died.

It also helped that I was older and more aware of my personal means of handling life's hard knocks. I had seventeen more years in recovery and had learned more about grief in watching Mom and how she handled the loss of her beloved husband of forty-three years.

Relief also came from new activities that unfolded in my search for healing and in many familiar activities I had done for years.

It all worked. It hasn't been easy, but I can say today I understand my grief process and respect it. From all this, I grew up to be the woman I always wanted to be.

I offer you a glimpse at my intimate thoughts and process for how I handled the biggest losses of my life. I used my personal journals as references for this book.

I hope this will help you arrive at that same point of healing that I did.

[1]*Codependency definition. 2017.* URL: http://www.mentalhealthamerica.net/co-dependency

HOW TO READ THIS BOOK

This book is a collection of stories, poetry, activities, and resources that helped me deal with my grief, so it doesn't need to be read in order.

Read the background stories about my dad and mom before the poetry or skip directly to the poetry that I wrote after Mom died.

Look at the Table of Contents and if a topic jumps out at you, go there and receive the comfort you need.

Choose what you need to help you.

It's all your choice. I like choice!

Chapter One

MEET DAD

Harold Laurence Horner
March 20, 1918 – January 6, 1996

People Instantly Know Me

In southeastern Colorado, Dad marked me.
    People instantly know me.

Is it the nose
    or the eyes?
    My movement on the dance floor?
    My smile?
    My lips?

Or is it everything about me?
    How do they know?

I burst with pride because I'm known as
    Harold Horner's daughter.

In the surrounding ranching
    and farming communities,
    people take one look at me and say,
    "Aren't you Harold Horner's youngest daughter?"

Many times I don't know who
    is asking the question,
    but with those words I always feel special,
    connected, and known,
    because I am proud to be:

Harold Horner's daughter.

DAD'S LIFE AND DEATH

My dad, Harold Horner, was a cowboy his whole life. He believed he was the luckiest man in the world because every day he did something he loved for a living. Side by side, he worked with his father on their family ranch, taking care of their cattle and horses.

As a child, Dad experienced a "touch of tuberculosis" that forced his family to move from the humid climate of Tulsa, Oklahoma to the high dry desert of southeastern Colorado, where he could—and did —thrive.

Even though his health was better overall, Dad also had asthma. For him it was agony—he wanted to be outside riding his horse and helping his dad on the ranch, but he was forced to be more careful than other kids.

Later in life, the asthma marked him as 4F (unfit for duty) when the draft came up for World War II. While he couldn't go to war, he found another way to serve: by helping out on ranches in the community whose sons did go to war. He had many fond memories of helping our neighbors then.

Granddad wasted no time and bought his seven-year-old a horse, and my dad took to horses as if he had ridden them his whole life. The day Granddad bought him a horse was the day his destiny was set. Dad

3

loved the cowboy way of life at once. He worked his whole life on that family ranch, doing the work he loved.

Dad's youth was a time of horseback riding, calving, helping his dad on the ranch, and hilarious times attending the small country school.

At this time, Granddad kept busy putting together our ranch when he wasn't working his job as a postal carrier. His postal job was a life-saver for them; because of that job, Granddad managed better than most during the depression. For other homesteaders surviving the depression was too hard a task. Our family ranch grew because Granddad bought out the homesteaders that couldn't make it.

One of Dad's favorite memories as a young man was when he helped Mose Russell move a herd of horses by horseback from south-eastern Colorado to Cimarron, New Mexico. Obviously it was a long trip, and Dad often recounted stories of their experience, mostly jokes about Mose's cooking.

When he was seventy years old, while gathering cattle on the ranch, Granddad got bucked off his horse and broke his pelvis. Several family members rode that day and saw this unscheduled rodeo—I was one of them. His doctor said he survived this horrible accident because of his physical fitness. Luckily, Granddad had always been an active man.

One year later in 1964, Dad got bucked off a horse and broke his hip. This altered his life; he had surgery, and a steel plate and screws repaired the damage. After a six- month period of recuperation, he rode horses again, but he walked with a limp for the rest of his life.

Later in his life, Dad enjoyed helping Bill Berg, his nephew, herd cattle on horseback from Folsom, New Mexico to the top of Johnson's Mesa to summer pasture. It reminded him of earlier times in his cowboy career when cowboys rode horses more often.

Dad's cowboy life came at the end of an era—when cowboys worked hard, rode horses, lived honest lives, and enjoyed a simpler life.

Dad loved the cowboy life, but he also loved his family. The love of his life was Elva Marie Dickerson Horner, my mom. He had three children from an earlier marriage: Fred, Larraine, and Sue. With my mother, he had two children: Harold (Bub) and me.

Dad's nickname for me was Shorty—I loved the sound of it. It was our special connection.

As a couple, my parents enjoyed a variety of passions: dancing, traveling, attending activities in our close-knit community and surrounding area, and loving their family.

For the most part, Dad was healthy until his seventies. By this time, he stopped riding horses and used his pickup to do most of the ranch work. A series of illnesses warned Mom and me that age was creeping up on him. For a couple years, he had yearly stays in the hospital for breathing issues.

Today, seventy isn't that old. But my dad was a heavy smoker most of his life. In 1988 he began to suffer the consequences; emphysema, asthma, and forty-plus years of heavy smoking had finally caught up with him.

In March of 1993, we celebrated his seventy-fifth birthday with a dinner and dance at the school gym in Branson for 200 guests. His breathing had worsened so much he couldn't dance the full circle of the dance floor.

The doctor diagnosed Dad with congestive heart failure that same summer, and he struggled with the restraints of the diet foisted upon him. He chose no treatment; that cowboy didn't want to spend his last years in a hospital.

Without any cause or warning, Dad's health changed two years later. I was teaching in Albuquerque, New Mexico when I received a frantic call from Mom: "He can't snap the snaps on his shirt. It seems he forgot how. Say nothing to your Dad, but please come as soon as you can!"

As soon as classes were over for the week, I drove home. I watched my seventy-eight-year-old father struggle with that simple task and many more. He looked at his fingers like they were foreign objects out of his control. I helped him finish snapping the snaps on the front of his shirt and cuffs and worried about his sudden change.

That evening we played our usual game of Rummy, and he had trouble identifying the numbers on the cards. I whispered, "Dad, that is a six, not a three." I didn't want to hurt his feelings and whispering softened the blow to us sitting at the breakfast bar. What was happening?

For the remainder of the weekend I scanned Mom's face, seeing the distress and fear. We knew something was wrong. He didn't seem to notice the changes, though, and that helped us manage this new stage in his life.

Mom took him to the doctor the next week.

After several weeks of testing and no solid answer, the diagnosis from a small town doctor was strange: Parkinson's disease, which made little sense because he had no tremors. The doctor never gave Dad a different diagnosis, and the medical world never solved the Parkinson's mystery.

After this, he progressed to the point of not being able to talk—his lips moved to form words but they just wouldn't come out, and his left hand curled up in a ball.

His intense, frustrated glaze locked in on me. His frightened eyes searched mine for the words. Sometimes I finished his sentences; other times I had no idea what he wanted to say. He struck the table with his clenched fist, more desperate each time it happened. Now he couldn't do the simplest tasks without help.

The internet of today wasn't in place then, so I had no place to research his strange symptoms. I struggled with Dad's changes that charged forward with no clear explanation. He suffered no pain; he just couldn't talk. His physical strength weakened.

His decline from August to November was drastic. By Thanksgiving, Mom needed help to handle his physical demands, so a neighbor came to help get Dad out of bed every morning and back in bed every evening. It became too much for Mom, isolated fifty miles from the nearest doctor and hospital.

Being Dad's main caretaker exhausted Mom, so we agreed to put Dad in the Trinidad nursing home at the first of December. Our plan was not long term, just a month break for her. She had such mixed feelings about our decision, but she needed time to regain her strength.

We worried that he might remember that his mother had died in this nursing home, but he didn't know where he was. He was slipping away for sure.

Dad's stay in that nursing home started out fine but ended with too many mistakes by the staff.

After several mishaps there, I met with the nursing home administrator about Dad's treatment and exploded, listing our concerns. Mom and I found Dad flat on his back often. He needed his head elevated at all times when he was in bed because of his breathing problems.

The final straw was finding him late one afternoon, laying flat again with his pants wrestled down to his knees because his diaper was dirty. He knew he had soiled himself, and we had no idea how long he had laid in that mess. We knew he'd felt the ugliness because he had tried to pull his pants down and get out of them. That's what bothered me the most.

With him not able to speak, we wondered if he knew what was happening. This proved he did, to some extent.

After a sad, tearful Christmas watching Dad in the nursing home, he got pneumonia, ended up in the hospital, and never left.

At this point, we had such limited options. We planned to put Dad back in the nursing home after his hospital stay until we found another solution, but the administrator refused to readmit Dad because of our meeting, so we had one choice—home health care.

That type of care was not available in 1995, fifty miles out in the country, but I found ways to do it. I had the hospital bed ordered and had a visiting nurse drive the long distance out to Branson three times a week. Mom and I hoped it might work.

I returned to Albuquerque to go back to work after the holiday break.

On January 6, 1996, Dad died in the hospital before we could bring him home. I wasn't there when Dad died. Uncle Tanky Doherty phoned me at roughly 2:00 A.M. that Dad was dying and I needed to come. A family friend, Modene Verquer, drove me to Trinidad, Colorado.

On the drive, I closed my eyes and prayed for Dad's healing but a deeper prayer emerged from my soul: a prayer for God's mercy and grace.

Snow covered the pastures as we sped by and power lines danced by my peripheral view. With urgency, I wanted to push the car faster down the road, but this winter wonderland blurred into a vast white haze. We arrived one hour too late.

A couple days after Dad's death, Bill Berg gave Mom a lengthy letter he wrote the night Dad died, identifying all that he loved about Dad. This letter touched us all.

His death certificate listed the cause of death as congestive heart failure. The Parkinson's diagnosis never showed up again.

I was sober eight years at the time. My recovery was a huge help through the loss of Dad. Dad and I had been so close my whole life. Ours was a volatile relationship with lots of disagreements over major issues, but we had reconciled and found a deep peace in our relationship.

This time was a blur. I helped Mom organize Dad's funeral, stayed a couple weeks after the funeral to help, and watched how she handled her loss. Her small frame sagged with the unbearable weight of it. Her eyes had lost their sparkle. She felt lost; her husband of forty-three years had died. Their ranching lifestyle had ensured that they were together all day long every day and she yearned for her life partner who had always been there.

MOM'S GRIEF PROCESS

Mom showed me how to grieve. She was fine one minute, then she would cry and be in her deep sorrow for a while, then it ended. This cycle repeated itself, and it worked for her. She also jumped right back into her life in our small ranching community.

I became Mom's primary caretaker long distance. I visited as often as I could, and we talked on the telephone. We spoke of Dad often.

At first, Mom bought herself lunch once a month and visited Dad's grave in Trinidad, Colorado. She talked to him like he was still there. It was their date. She yearned to be near him.

Her involvement in her church supported her through her loss. She prayed and cried. Her faith grew during this time, and she drew strength from her God.

Mom danced alone around the living room to *Molly B's Polka Party* on Saturday nights—dancing had been a regular part of their lives. Then she listened to old country music shows to help her deal with the loss of her dance partner on the night they danced the most: Saturday!

Her attendance at activities in our small ranching community continued—she didn't stop living! Mom attended her craft club. She enjoyed basketball games where she sat in her favorite seat and hollered for the Bearcats, like she always had. Now she sat with Doris Goff instead of Dad.

I watched Mom and took note.

She took her time to get rid of Dad's clothes and personal items. That gave her the opportunity to gift many of Dad's clothes to her great-grandson when he came to visit a few years ago. His eyes lit up when Mom asked him if he wanted them. He wanted them when no one else in the family did, and Mom loved that.

Anniversaries were hard—their wedding anniversary, his birthday, and the anniversary of his death. What made these days harder for Mom were calls on those memorable days from well-intentioned family and friends who then talked about everything else but Dad. She told me she so often wanted to scream, "Talk about Harold, please! Ask me questions. Remember fun times we had. Speak his name. I need to hear his name."

I have spent all of my adult years within four to five hours of my parents, so we were close. Dad and I started a Christmas tradition many years ago. He loved it when "his two girls" dressed alike, so every year, I bought his Christmas presents for Mom and me: an outfit alike.

Preparing for our first Christmas without Dad, Mom stated in a tearful whisper, "You don't have to buy our Christmas outfits this year." I continued buying them every year until she died—a small piece of Dad kept with us over the years.

Mom healed; she grieved, and she continued to live and enjoy her altered life without Dad. She managed the family ranch and did a fine job. She traveled. She was most happy when her house was full and she was busy in the kitchen preparing a meal for her family or friends. Mom had transmuted every tear, every lonely night in bed, every time she heard their song, "Four in the Morning," and wept, and every sorrow into a life well lived.

MY PROCESS — NO POETRY WHEN DAD DIED

When my dad died, I didn't write poetry to get clarity, to heal myself, nor to see the events of my life as a part of my process. I wrote but not to deal with my loss.

I focused on Mom—that's what I did, and I danced and worked.

We talked often about Dad, our loss, and our grief. I realized these conversations were important for both of us to heal. I learned that from her and relished her wisdom—I listened. Her tender care of herself demonstrated to me how to do this mysterious thing so many don't understand how to do: grieve.

Time healed Mom. She managed her grief and lived seventeen years without Dad, in relative comfort and happiness.

I wanted that for myself when she passed. Here's how I did that.

Chapter Two

LET'S CELEBRATE MOM

Elva Marie Dickerson Horner
September 24, 1928 – March 23, 2013

HERE'S YOUR LIFE, ELVA MARIE DICKERSON HORNER

Larada Horner

A poem in three voices read at Mom's seventy-fifth birthday celebration in Clearlake, California, read by Connie Horner Herron, Andy Horner, and Cheryl Horner-Christensen in 2003. The information in this poem was used for Mom's eulogy.

February 13, 1919 a young couple rode horseback to marry
    Virgil and Tresia
    Nine months later Willa Lee came
    Nine years later Elva Marie was born on September 24, 1928.

Your story starts here!

Youngest child,
    Dirt floors in your home,
    Ma and Pa lived close
    Violin lessons you wanted so much

Donald Lujan called you "Squeaky,"
which ended your violin lessons abruptly.

A move to Raton, New Mexico from Des Moines, New Mexico
when you were in the eighth grade.
In high school you hung out with the country kids from
Johnson Mesa.
You went to Denver to see the play, "Othello," and were mystified.
Hughie and Willie were married and along came Janet.
You played with her like a doll.

And you loved to dance.
A certain cowboy caught your eye at a dance.
You noticed his different dance style.

At the Robin Hood in Raton, New Mexico, he crossed the dance floor
     toward you.
     You knew he was going to ask you to dance,
     and you panicked,
     The romance of a lifetime started that night
     with Harold Horner.

You dated;
     you danced!
     You got thrown out of the Crystal Lounge because you were
     underage,
     but Harold returned to you
     when you turned twenty-one.

You were married on August 28, 1951 in Raton, New Mexico.
     Your married life that would span forty-three years had begun.
     You immediately became a stepmother
     to three small children:
     Fred, Larraine, and Sue.

As newlyweds you moved in
     with your in-laws in Branson, Colorado.
     You experienced a small town tradition—chivaree
     Short-sheeted the beds,
     Removed labels off all the canned goods,
     A wet wheelbarrow ride for the new bride.

Your first home was bought from the Stephenson's
     lock, stock, and barrel.

On May 25, 1952, Harold Virgil arrived;
     On June 27, 1953, Teresa Larada appeared

thirteen months apart!
Your family intact!!!

Lots of life happened in that small country town through the years.
    The children grew—Dad remembers coming home from La Junta
    and
    caught you in the rocking chair with a baby in each arm.
    Your arms were numb!
    You painted bright red lips for the thin-lipped Larada.
    She looked like a clown.
    You spanked Bub and Larada with a wooden spoon.
    You shampooed Larada's hair and sculpted it to stand up straight
    and tall.
    Larada marveled at your sculpture of hair

Bub caught his hand in the washing machine wringer.
    You ran next door to Edna Fry for help,
    left Bub and Larada crying.
    Edna hit the release button
    and Bub was freed.

School filled the fall and winter months with basketball, dances, and
    cheerleading.
    Spring was calving, baseball, and branding.
    Summer was Little League, horses, 4-H, and our county fair,
    our one family vacation every year.
    And so many children at our house all year long
    because you
    made them feel so welcome!

Marriages—Ron, Fred, and Lela joined our family!

Nine grandchildren came:
    Connie, Andy, Cheryl,
    Jeff, Wade, Ellen,
    Jason, Travis, and Blake.

Eleven great-grandchildren
    and one on the way.

You cherished family get-togethers and holidays.
    Granddad Horner loved to have family
    get-togethers at our house because of
    your cooking and hospitality!

After Granddad Horner died,
    you became Dad's right-hand man,
    able to do anything on the ranch—
    You worked hard and right along side Dad,
    Then you came home and prepared lunch!

You and Dad enjoyed a remarkable relationship of
    shared interests:
    you danced, traveled,
    worked together, and loved people.

You lovingly cared for Dad to the end,
    heartbroken and sick when he died.

You have taken care of yourself these
    last few years admirably.

Your interest varies.

You're an avid sports' fan of all of the Branson sports;
    you yelled loudly at basketball games
    with Mary Arguello.
    You now sit in the same place
    high in the gym bleachers
    every game with Doris Goff.

You have been involved in the Branson Community—
    Home Demonstration Club,
    now Craft club
    and Community Club
    working through PTA for many years.
    You helped start the Annual Junior High
    Basketball tournament.

In the '70s you got interested in genealogy
    and researched both the
    Dickerson
    and
    Horner
    sides extensively.
    You cherish your black genealogy book
    with all the important dates
    and names.

Girlfriends have been a part of your life forever:
    Ellen Berry in high school;
    Clara Warner, Nancy Salas, and Mokey McMillan years ago;
    Helen Waldroup, Betty Clark, and Rose Ward now.

A TIME TO GROW UP

After Dad died,
    you were baptized and became a faithful member
    of the Des Moines Methodist church,
    attending every Sunday with Bill and Janet.
    Afterwards, the regular group ate lunch and chatted.

All of us have evidence of your beautiful handiwork: afghans, quilts,
    Christmas ornaments and more.

In 1999, you and Larada took a trip to eastern Europe to find
    information about your great-grandfather Ulbig.
    It was a trip of a lifetime.

Often when we are with you, we get the privilege of
    hearing your laughter,
    so rich and inviting
    seeing your blue eyes twinkle.

Here are some memories that make your blue eyes sparkle:

- The first time Harold Horner asked you to dances
- Connie made a milkshake with you, and it ended up all over
  the floor.
- Andy looked through the Remington cowboy book together
  with you and made up stories.
- Cheryl drew the "God Don't Make Junk" picture for you,
  and you sat the whole time watching her draw. You still
  have it on your refrigerator.
- The twins loved going to the trailer and playing baseball
  with you.

Mom, what a wonderful life we celebrate today—seventy-five glorious
years!

THE FRAGRANT LILAC OF MY LIFE!

A poem I wrote as her Christmas present in 2003, also read at Mom's service.

She is Mom,
but she is more!

A knot chokes my throat as
I look at her profile so familiar—
an outline of nose and chin
etched in my memory.
She's the fragrant lilac of my life!

Seventy-five years she celebrated this year!

I watch her walk
cautious, after cataract surgery
brushing a toe, a foot forward gingerly
and awkward,
Her life changing before me.

I sit next to her
and laugh
Two little girls enjoying each other,
not mother and daughter.

Her teasing causes
a giggle so deep
it rumbles in my
belly and my childhood.

She has often made me laugh
a playmate that stirs
a ridiculous side of me,
My first playmate.

We wrestle,
the laughter goes deeper.
The joy I feel in our
physical contact rings
heavenly.

Her this close to me—
I smell her sweet scent,
a mixture of life,
Love, pain, and sweat.

Our laughter continues
and I smile deeply.
My heart smiles
in remembrance.

This is the woman
who carried me close
to her heart,
and we still live there
when we laugh.

Chapter Three

MOM'S DECLINE

Mom dealt with numerous health concerns her whole adult life. She had her gallbladder removed when she was a young mother, suffered with blood clots in her legs and took a blood thinner (Coumadin) for years, and had a thyroid problem and needed medicine for it until she passed away. In the late 1980s, Mom fell off of a haystack while helping Dad and fractured her wrist—the result of being a rancher's wife and osteoporosis. In her last years, she had several bouts with diverticulitis and had acid reflux.

1996 – 2012

After Dad died in January 1996, Mom experienced unusual symptoms: her cheeks became bright red like she had ran a mile; she had itchy, red blotches on her legs; and she didn't feel well, but she couldn't put her finger on the cause.

That autumn, Mom saw a specialist in Pueblo, Colorado and was diagnosed with polycythemia vera. Mayo clinic states this is "a slow-growing type of blood cancer in which your bone marrow makes too many red blood cells. Polycythemia vera may also result in production of too many of the other types of blood cells—white blood cells and platelets."[2]

Because of this blood disorder, she endured years of monthly phle-botomies. Mom never knew what to expect. The nurses often failed at finding her tiny veins, so she got stuck several times, making the whole ordeal even more terrible for her. Sometimes when they did success-fully find a vein, blood gushed everywhere. She feared these monthly appointments even as some of the capable nurses became loving friends of hers from spending so much time together.

She continued the phlebotomy routine for twelve years, until a new hematologist prescribed an increased dose of a chemotherapy pill, which eliminated the horrible monthly blood draws. The drawback, the doctor warned her, was that this disease might flip flop into leukemia. The possibility that it would became her greatest fear.

But it wasn't until sixteen years after Dad died that her health changed drastically.

November 22 – 25, 2012

It was on Thanksgiving Day 2012, when I noticed a change in my mom—she looked thinner. The family—Mom, of course, Aunt Willie, my niece Connie and her three children, and my husband, Lin, and I—was gathered in Branson and Mom was cooking her usual delicious feast. Mom's favorite holidays centered around big meals she'd cooked with loved ones seated around her round table. Her favorite ending to the day included playing games with lots of laughter.

Our normal routines dictated that holiday's weekend activities—an excursion to the ranch during the day with lots of exploring of our favorites spots. The group stopped at the canyon's rim, searching for wildlife. We walked down to the edge of the canyon to the Coronado cave and hunted arrowheads. That night, we played lots of games—Apples to Apples and a fun domino game called PIP.

We delighted in our holiday traditions, but Mom lacked any appetite for the big feast she'd prepared. I observed a decline that weekend in her eating and realized this was the reason for her loss of weight.

In the weeks after, between Thanksgiving and Christmas, I phoned Mom daily. When I questioned how she was doing, she'd often say,

"Worn out and no energy." My concern only increased when she answered that way. It was so different than her usual response.

December 22, 2012

I had shoulder surgery, and Mom wanted to come and help after my operation, but she wasn't well, so I reassured her that Lin would take great care of me. The surgery went well.

December 24, 2012

Lin and I planned to drive home on Christmas Eve, but he woke up sick, so we laid over a day. It helped me recuperate too because I was just two days away from surgery.

December 25, 2012

We rousted up early Christmas morning and drove the four-and-a-half-hour trip home. Mom's sister, Willie was with her, so she hadn't been alone.

Her lack of appetite had worsened since Thanksgiving, so her hematologist prescribed Megestrol, an appetite stimulant. She looked tired and worn out—worse than Thanksgiving.

We opened our gifts and celebrated our holiday together. We enjoyed a lazy Christmas afternoon and the meal Mom had prepared. Her cooking used to be the thrill of her life, but now it became a chore.

December 26, 2012

In the morning, Connie telephoned to say she, her fiancé, and her family of three wanted to come over from Texas the following day. Normally Connie's visits elated Mom, but she nearly fainted.

I will never forget the bewildered expression on her face. I grabbed the telephone before she dropped it and exclaimed, "We are so excited to have you come and visit." But Connie had picked up on the reluctance in tone and realized there was something unusual and wrong. Later she questioned me about Mom's response.

My cousin and her husband, Bill and Janet Berg, celebrated with us, and we had a nice dinner and visit.

December 27, 2012
Early in the morning, Mom drove us to Trinidad to pick up groceries because I couldn't drive due to my recent shoulder surgery. More relaxed than the day before, she smiled about this serendipitous adventure ahead of us. We ate breakfast at one of her favorite cafes and giggled our way through the grocery shopping.

Mom, Lin, and I enjoyed the visit with Connie and her family. As we rallied around Mom's round table each evening and played our favorite games, screams of happiness and laughter filled the night. We took daily trips to the ranch to visit our favorite sites: the Coronado cave, the corrals and the edges overlooking the canyon searching for wildlife.

That evening, Mom and Kaylea Raye, Connie's youngest daughter, pulled a practical joke with whipped cream on Lin while he napped in the living room. They dabbed whipped cream on his nose while he slept in a recliner. The participants in the mischief celebrated their successful trick; the rest of us enjoyed their fun but knew we could be next. Mom loved practical jokes—everyone knew not to sleep in the living room with her there.

December 28, 2012
That night, we sat around the living room telling stories of the past. Any other time, Mom refused being videoed, but that evening I recorded both Aunt Willie and Mom telling a couple old stories. Mom jumped right in, no objections to my camera, with one of her favorite childhood stories. Her mother had peered out their front door and realized a hobo was coming a little too close to their house. She was afraid he was going to try something, so she hollered at their dog. But the dog was tied up to a washtub outside. When her mother called out, the dog jumped up and chased the hobo, dragging the tub over a wire fence and destroying it.

December 29, 2012

Connie and her family left at noon after our fun time together—no problems at all. Lin offered to vacuum after they left and made several comments about how bad the vacuum was working. Mom got mad about his comments, but the vacuum wasn't picking up the dirt. This was the start of her strange bad mood, which worsened in time.

That night we watched all of Mom's favorite Saturday night music shows on RFD-TV, enjoying country and western music and lots of polkas.

December 30, 2012

Later in the afternoon after Aunt Willie had left, Mom, Lin, and I watched a Broncos game. Lin spent the afternoon flipping between two games during the commercials. Mom sat in her recliner and didn't utter a word—her silence screamed that something bothered her, but I had no idea what. Afterward, Mom told my brother that she became upset because she couldn't tell which game we were watching, but she refused to explain this to us.

At this point, Mom's voice became hoarse but she appeared okay.

New Year's Eve loomed ahead of us—what should we do? Lin and I discussed possible special places to go in Trinidad, but Mom got annoyed with us over our suggestions. She preferred to eat at McDonald's because of the return of the McRib sandwich; we wanted a more special celebration. This was only our second New Year's Eve since we had married.

December 31, 2012

Lin and I won the restaurant decision and spent a sad New Year's Eve with Mom and Scott Warner, a lifelong friend, at an Italian restaurant in Trinidad. The restaurant we chose had singing waiters who entertained us with their musical performances. What might have been a delightful, fun evening labored on and on with Mom's anger evident. Her hoarseness continued, but she continued to deny any problem.

I had a sleepless night, upset about Mom.

January 1, 2013

We watched the traditional New Year's Day TV: the Rose Bowl parade and then lots of college football games. Mom continued her bad mood all day: she fumed, kept her distance, and refused to talk to me. This wasn't like her. I questioned her that night, but she refused to acknowledge a problem.

Again, I hardly slept, worrying about Mom.

January 2, 2013

Mom was still angry as we prepared to leave for the trip back home. Our relationship had its issues, but her displeasure didn't make sense. Her hoarseness worsened, and she continued to assure us she was fine, but I knew in my heart that nothing was fine.

As part of my morning routine for the last six years, I called her every day while I drove to work. As we stood at the door to leave, she stared past me and stated, "You don't need to call me every day any longer." I walked to our car in tears.

After we left, it took her eight hours to take down her Christmas decorations when it should have taken half that time—she felt drained and this didn't make sense.

Worried, I phoned Jackie Mock, a friend who helped take care of Mom, and she expressed that she and her husband had observed a difference in Mom and her behavior over the last two months. After arriving home, I researched the appetite stimulant prescribed and talked to Mom about the possible side effects: mood swings, an allergic reaction of not breathing, and blood clots.

Her attitude toward me softened once I wasn't there—she appreciated my concern and called her hematologist to question the appetite stimulant, and he agreed to stop the medicine.

I called her every day as usual, even though she'd told me not to. In fact, I talked to her several times a day. Her hoarse voice worsened.

For two weeks, she remained at home and attempted to medicate herself. Jackie and she called her doctor, and he suggested using a vaporizer, so she had one going in each room of her house, but she still grew sicker.

January 13, 2013

On the drive home after my recovery meeting, I called Mom. At first she sounded better, but she became hoarse as we talked. When she began to repeat questions, my concern grew.

January 15, 2013

The progression moved fast. Mom woke at 3:00 A.M. and couldn't breathe, which scared her and pushed her toward going to the hospital.

Because of her laryngitis, she couldn't talk on the phone, so I had to call Jackie to see how she was doing. I so worried about Mom—she was really depressed and her condition wasn't improving. In the meantime, I researched assisted-living facilities in Albuquerque, preparing for the possible future.

January 17, 2013

After not talking to Mom since January 13, I couldn't resist, so I called her. Her voice still sounded raspy, and she had lost five pounds —that scared me. She whispered, "I can't eat."

I knew we had to do something. Bub, Jackie, and I preferred that Mom go to the hospital in Pueblo, Colorado, but she refused because she wanted to go to Raton, New Mexico.

That afternoon, they hospitalized Mom in Raton after two weeks of dealing with the hoarseness and severe loss of appetite. When she was admitted, she weighed 109, almost twenty pounds less than her normal weight, a gradual downhill progression that began before Christmas.

Mom was extremely anemic from what the doctor's thought was internal bleeding, but no one knew the cause. The Coumadin level in her blood was high, too. Jackie and my cousin Janet played a big part in helping Mom. We exchanged many phone calls, trying to decide the best treatment for her.

Mom experienced her first and second blood transfusions that first night in the hospital. Afterwards, she felt strengthened and better but still hoarse and coughing.

One of the doctors talked about putting a scope down her throat, then he postponed it due to the danger posed by the blood thinner she took.

January 18, 2013

During our morning phone conversation on Friday, I told Mom I had Monday off because of Martin Luther King Day, so Lin and I were coming to Raton to see her tomorrow.

The first thing she said to me was, "Can I go home with you to Tijeras?" Delighted, I gave her a resounding "Yes."

On the drive home after work, I realized I had missed my physical therapy appointment for my shoulder. When I got home to Lin, I broke down and sobbed—it was all too much. I felt overwhelmed with all my worry about Mom.

January 19, 2013

Early in the morning, Lin and I drove to Raton. When we arrived, the doctor said they were ready to release Mom but still had no idea where she was bleeding internally. She looked frail and sick!

It shocked us that they would release her in that state, so I challenged the doctor, wanting a more definitive diagnosis before I took her fifty miles away from a hospital. I also reminded him it hadn't been twenty-four hours since her last blood transfusion. So they decided to keep her one more night. Mom had her third blood transfusion in two days that night—what was going on?

Timidly, Mom asked again, "Can I go home with you to Tijeras?" Relief flooded me. I was afraid she might have changed her mind. We needed to find a doctor who would find the solution, and I needed to be with her!

Her symptoms stumped the physicians in Raton, and her blood count continued downward. She had a bad cough so she received breathing treatments, too.

January 20, 2013

The doctors still didn't know what was going on with Mom, but they released her on Sunday. The doctor who admitted Mom refused to see me and answer my questions face-to-face. She said nothing had changed since the last time we had talked and sent the answers to my questions by the nurse.

We took Mom home to Branson to pick up her clothes and personal belongings. I did laundry and prepared to find doctors in Albuquerque for Mom.

While we got everything ready to go, Betty Clark, a neighbor, came to check on Mom. As they visited, they both told me that they had the same primary care doctor in Raton, and he never touched them when he checked them. They both lamented over that! I couldn't believe it.

January 21, 2013

I spent the day booking two doctor appointments in Albuquerque for Mom. I found a primary care physician and an ear, eye, and throat specialist to deal with her throat and breathing issues. Mom relaxed for the day, but I knew she didn't feel well because she allowed me to do lots of things for her that she normally did herself. She did pack her clothes though.

January 22, 2013

I took an extra day off so we didn't have to rush back home.

As we left Branson on that sad morning, Mom paused at the front gate and gazed back at her house, crying. "I wonder if I will ever be back here," she'd said. I helped her get in the back seat and watched her in the mirror—her tears fell as we pulled out of the driveway. I choked back my tears, wondering the same thing.

Mom was hospitalized three times in two different Albuquerque hospitals after that.

January 23, 2013

First, we tackled her throat issues at an ear, eye, and throat specialist office where she was treated by a caring physician's assistant immediately. The PA did a scope of her throat and found a lesion. He scheduled a second appointment to deal with it.

January 24, 2013

We met with a primary care physician who sensed the urgency of Mom's health needs. Mom whimpered as she shared her mysterious medical woes. The doctor touched her shoulder and consoled her. I don't remember his words but his touch and gentle spirit convinced us that we had found someone who would listen.

When he left the room, Mom smiled at me through her tears. "He's a good doctor. He just touched me." She started having stomach cramps in his office and became nauseated.

This doctor worried about Mom taking Coumadin and her blood loss, so he gave her a prescription to replace the Coumadin—an injection for blood thinner in her stomach. He asked me if I could give Mom the shot. Necessity forced me to do it. I remember seeing Mom stretched out on her bed in our guest room with her eyes begging me. She raised her blouse and stated, "Do it!"

She realized this task exceeded my comfort level, but I would have done anything for her. She brushed my hand with hers and encouraged me, and I gave her the shot, with tears spilling down my cheeks. I only gave one shot because everything became complicated.

That evening, Mom vomited.

January 25, 2013

Mom's new primary care physician admitted her into the hospital, nine days after her hospital visit in Raton. One of the quarrelsome physicians in Raton had badgered Mom, saying she didn't need to be in the hospital and stated, "If you went to a hospital in Albuquerque, they wouldn't admit you." A mistaken diagnosis!

[2]*Polycythemia vera definition.* *2017.* URL: http://www.mayoclinic.org/diseases-conditions/polycythemia-vera/basics/definition/con-20031013

Chapter Four

MOM'S DIAGNOSIS CHANGED HER LIFE

January 26, 2013

In this initial hospitalization in Albuquerque, I became a patient advocate for Mom because her first assigned doctor gave her a colonoscopy without any sedative. When she returned to the room after the procedure, she bawled and felt ashamed. "I screamed like a baby, it hurt so bad, and he did nothing to help me. During the procedure he visited with the nurse about his personal life. It was horrible." Mom's nurse and I shed tears as we hugged her. I couldn't believe this.

As we consoled her, Mom cried. "The doctor said he does not give a sedative to any of his elderly patients." The nurse insisted this wasn't true, and all of the floor nurses agreed. She did have another blood transfusion, and she felt energized by it.

From the colonoscopy, the doctor decided Mom's diverticulitis caused the internal bleeding. Finally, we had an explanation.

I attempted to work with other doctors assigned to Mom. I considered myself a warrior, battling the doctors and the system.

We did have one pleasant experience with one doctor there. He identified that Mom had pulmonary hypertension as a result of smoking, which she never did. My dad was a chain smoker and many of their friends smoked, but Mom didn't, so her condition came from second-hand smoke. The doctor wondered which came first—the pulmonary hypertension or the polycythemia vera.

We mused about this new diagnosis—maybe the use of oxygen would replace the chemo pill and/or the phlebotomies.

At this hospital, Mom's INR number and Coumadin dosage became a major medical focus for the doctors. According to Allina Health web site, an INR (International Normalized Ratio) number is a number that identifies "how fast the blood clots in patients receiving oral anticoagulant medication."[3]

Mom stayed in this hospital for ten days.

February 2, 2013

The hideous medical system dragged out Mom's dismissal from the hospital for six hours; after mishap after mishap, I finally got her home at 6:00 P.M. We left that place with no real answers to Mom's escalating health decline and were determined not to return to that hospital.

When I returned home that evening from my recovery meeting, Mom's cheeks were bright red. I checked her temperature—102 degrees. This was something new! Her evening fevers started.

All through February, she spiked fevers in the evening, and I didn't know what to do. I have no children, so I Googled what to do: wet washcloths on her forehead, Tylenol, and ice chips to nibble on.

One night I gave Mom a haircut. She began to shake uncontrollably. She had a one hundred degree fever and shook for over an hour. The fever went up to 102, even with the treatment I'd found online.

The fevers disappeared in the morning, only to return that night or the next. The nightly fevers exhausted her, leaving her uncomfortably soaked and causing sleeplessness, and I struggled with what to do.

Her primary care doctor added visits to the "Coumadin Clinic"—a weekly check to see what Mom's INR number was and then adjust her Coumadin dosage. That's what her Raton primary care doctor didn't do. He didn't check her INR number for six months, and her Coumadin level was outrageous when she was admitted to the Raton hospital.

The nurse practitioner at the Coumadin clinic decided on a more specific dosage, altering the amounts each day. On her first visit to the clinic, her INR number tested 1.6—up from 1.3 on Saturday in Raton, an encouraging change.

February 9, 2013

Mom's fever hit 104 degrees. She spent the evening with a wet washcloth on her forehead, chewing on ice chips, and taking Tylenol. It took all evening for the fever to go down. Her hollow, fearful eyes searched mine for help and an explanation. What to do?

I cried myself to sleep that night but had a plan for the next day.

February 10, 2013

Because of the high fever the night before, I took Mom to Urgent Care in Albuquerque by 8:15 A.M. She had pneumonia, so maybe that explained the high fevers. We gladly welcomed a reprieve from the fevers, but it sadly only lasted a short period.

February 11, 2013

We'd had to put her throat problem on the back burner before, but that day Mom saw the ear, eye, and throat specialist to deal with the lesion. He decided not to do a scope because it wasn't cancer.

February 14, 2013

We celebrated the Coumadin clinic visit today—her INR number was 2.4, the highest it had been in a month. We didn't have to come back for two weeks.

Mom and I met Lin at Burger Boy in Cedar Crest, New Mexico for our Valentine's Day dinner and had a nice time.

The fever returned that night, shocking us. Mom was on antibiotics. Why did she have a fever of 102.5?

I bought Mom and Lin chocolates and cards, but it felt so hollow because my worry and fear were mounting.

At this time, Mom questioned me often, "Will I ever be able to go home?" I repeated the same answer each time, "Yes, you will!" I really believed she would get better, go home, and resume her independent life.

February 18, 2013

Mom's primary care physician requested a major blood test, so I took Mom to have blood drawn. These professionals poked her four times, and three of the workers tried to draw her blood but couldn't. The last one hurt her. They ended up taking two small bottles of blood —twice the size of miniature alcohol bottles.

The fevers continued and now Mom had to deal with nausea and couldn't eat. Whatever was wrong with her was worsening. I have never felt so helpless and defeated in my life.

The repeated fevers baffled her primary care physician and hematologist, but I had more access to her hematologist on the telephone during the evening than her other physician.

February 21, 2013

Mom didn't have a fever during the evening but must have had one during the night because she woke up with her gown wet. That was different.

My cousin Janet brought up Mom's stationary bike, hoping the exercise might help her.

February 22, 2013

On another late night phone call to Mom's hematologist, I ended up talking to his partner. We chatted about Mom's repetitive, strange high fevers, and he asked me when did she have her last bone marrow biopsy. I replied, "Never," and he gasped. This offered us a new direction.

February 23, 2013

After another phone call to Mom's primary care doctor and lamenting to his nurse about our frustration with Mom's fevers, he pulled the rug out from beneath us saying, "I don't know what to do!" He said if she has another fever, take her to the emergency room, and he canceled our next appointment. He stopped responding to any of my messages. He bowed out! What were we supposed to do then?

February 25, 2013

Mom was really sick that evening—it scared me. When I went to bed, I cried and cried.

I didn't know what to do since her primary care physician pulled out. She was more frail and despondent. She lost weight because she couldn't eat. It was terrifying!

February 26, 2013

Mom's primary care physician's nurse called and told me I heard the doctor wrong. She apologized and said he suggested finding an Infectious Disease Specialist.

I got a strange call from Mom's hematologist's office in Pueblo, and the nurse said none of Mom's symptoms were caused by the poly-cythemia vera. I told her about the conversation I had with the hema-tologist's partner about a bone marrow biopsy. She called back and said they would connect us with a doctor at the New Mexico Cancer Center —finally some active support from that office!

February 27, 2013

After work, we returned to the Coumadin clinic and her INR number was 4.9—more than twice what it was two weeks earlier. This dosage of Coumadin worked on her blood count, but Mom's nausea worsened.

February 28, 2013

We returned to the ear, eye, and throat specialist, and the lesion was healed. He talked to us a lot about acid reflux and what to do about it.

The hematologist from Pueblo hadn't called yet about connecting us to the New Mexico Cancer Center. I thought the hematologist was going to make the appointment, but maybe I misunderstood him.

March 1, 2013

Mom had a horrible night. She ate tomato soup for lunch and became nauseous. When I got home from work, she was moaning. She had a fever and then vomited. I slept downstairs with Mom that night, so worried about her.

I had been reluctant to take Mom to the emergency room in Albuquerque, concerned about all the germs that would be in the waiting room this time of year. How long we'd have to wait also worried me because Mom was so frail. So I came up with a plan on how to get her admitted easily. I vacillated between going to Urgent Care or the emergency room.

March 2, 2013

We rose early this Saturday morning, and Lin and I had Mom at the emergency room of the other big hospital in Albuquerque by 9:00 A.M., and it worked. There were only two people in the waiting room, so they admitted her quickly with little wait time.

Immediately they did a CT scan and another blood transfusion. The doctor said she was seeping blood somehow, even though it wasn't showing in her stool.

I mentioned a bone marrow biopsy and an infectious disease specialist, and the doctor thought they were good ideas.

Mom had several visitors that first day in the hospital: Jackie Mock, Rose Ward, and Carlos Sandoval from home and her nephew Larry Waldroup.

I found a purple teddy bear in the gift shop downstairs, so I bought it for Mom—she loved sleeping with it.

March 3, 2013

We received the results of the CT scan—an enlarged spleen—so they scheduled the bone marrow biopsy for the next day.

The two units of blood and the visitors perked Mom up, so we did a couple Skype sessions with my brother, Bub, and his granddaughter, Summer, in California. Mom loved it.

Hopefully the information from the CT scan and the bone marrow biopsy test would tell us what was wrong.

March 4, 2013

An oncologist came on board, and Mom endured the bone marrow biopsy. The technicians allowed me to stay in the room during the procedure—they came to her room and did it. They said I could stay if I focused on Mom and not the procedure—they probably didn't want me to faint. I knelt at her head and held her hand. She squeezed hard, and I talked to her through the whole ordeal.

March 5, 2013

The oncologist diagnosed Mom with myelofibrosis which Mayo Clinic defines as "a serious bone marrow disorder that disrupts your body's normal production of blood cells. The result is extensive scarring in your bone marrow, leading to severe anemia, weakness, fatigue, and often, an enlarged spleen and liver."[4] But she offered no explanation to us.

I asked the doctor for more information about the disease. She did not use the "L-word" but used a metaphor: "It's like there's a fire in her blood factory and it's destroyed. There's scar tissue, and she's not producing the right blood cells." I called Lin, and he researched the diagnosis and called me back and said, "It's leukemia." Later her oncologist confirmed this.

I realized that Mom didn't know this mysterious disease was a type of leukemia—Mom's worst fears come true. I faced telling her the truth. So I looked her in the eyes and whispered, "Mom, myelofibrosis is a type of leukemia."

We both broke down and cried. She questioned me, "How long do I have to live?" At that point, I didn't know. Then she whispered, "I don't want to linger." I invited a gentle chaplain from the hospital to visit

Mom, and he consoled her by validating her fear and led her in a peaceful visualization. It comforted her at this stressful time.

I had to go back to work for the afternoon, but when I returned in the evening, Mom was nauseous. Her nurse whispered in my ear, "All she wanted was you." I sobbed!

The nausea continued, so the doctor added a nausea medication to her regime of medicine.

March 6, 2013

I got up at 5:15 A.M. so I could go by Walmart and buy Mom bigger panties—she was so swollen because of the enlarged spleen.

Mom was eating breakfast and something stuck in her throat, causing her to vomit all down the front of her gown; it happened quickly and it embarrassed her. She was nauseous for the rest of the day.

The oncologist conferred with us about Mom's treatment, giving me an application for Jakafi, an experimental drug costing $10,000 a month. They needed to do a gene study to see if she had the JAKS gene. If she did, then we could apply to Medicare to get the drug started and hopefully stop this insane disease.

I asked to talk privately to the oncologist to see if she was withholding any information. She assured me that she didn't do that. I asked her about Mom's prognosis. She said there were two possibilities: "maybe she won't make it out of the hospital or maybe she'll feel better after a couple months on the drug." Nothing too reassuring!

What a full day it was. In the afternoon, the doctor put in a filter so Mom could stop the Coumadin. As we waited, I asked her if she was scared. Immediately she responded, "No."

I questioned her because I was.

She smiled and replied, "Because you're here with me." Her response melted my heart. The procedure took longer than we thought, but we were relieved that she was off Coumadin.

They gave Mom two more blood transfusions.

At this point, Mom's care-taking demands overwhelmed me: watching what she ate and managing the medical team and her medication and the numerous blood transfusions. Her bruised, swollen right arm hurt from having blood drawn so often. I labored with keeping track of her various doctors because the hospital changed them weekly, and on top of all of this, I still worked full time.

At 8:00 P.M. after such a full day, the evening nurse commented, "Look at your mom's arms. They're so swollen and bruised. Let's get some ice on them."

Mom never complained about her level of pain or discomfort.

Shocked, I realized the day nurse mentioned it hours ago, but in the rush of the day and of getting the filter, I neglected relieving the swelling and her arm worsened. In shock, I wondered, "What happened to the day, to the care of my mother?"

Sobbing on the drive home, I called Bub. He offered to fly out and help.

March 7, 2013

Bub and his youngest daughter, Cheryl, flew to Albuquerque—I was at my wit's end.

Their presence relieved me! Mom needed them there, too. We worked as a solid unit. Cheryl stayed for five days and Bub stayed until the end. Due to Cheryl's astute observation, we realized Mom was having trouble swallowing, which became a key fact.

After Cheryl's observation, one of Mom's doctors ordered a swallow test that identified major swallowing problems for her. They adjusted her diet to a soft one, and it became easier for her to eat. Ice cream became her mainstay, but I still battled with her to eat. Food didn't taste good to her, and her enlarged spleen put pressure on her internal organs, causing severe back pain and major swelling in her abdomen; therefore, she refused to eat.

As the disease progressed, she coped with severe nausea. Mom's swollen spleen crowded out the other organs. After changing the combinations of medications, the palliative nurse got a mixture of medication that kept Mom relatively comfortable.

I had never heard of palliative care before. She encouraged us not do the Jakafi treatment and talked more about keeping Mom comfortable. She also mentioned hospice for the first time; I wasn't ready to think about that because I was still fighting to keep Mom alive.

Looking back, I think what she was trying to do was spare us from the disappointment that the trial drug ended up being. Also I got the feeling that she felt the oncologists were using Mom as a guinea pig with the drug, and she didn't want that for Mom. In denial of the severity of Mom's condition, I believed the two older oncologists' statement that she could get better on Jakafi.

I kept asking doctors for more information. Once, one of the older oncologists told a nurse to talk to me about Jakafi because I knew more than he did. I was shocked—I only knew what they had told me and what I had researched.

I felt like they were withholding information. I found out that the oncologist was. The rotating primary doctor assigned to us that week told me that Mom's bone marrow was totally dry and not producing any red blood cells. He also shared that she would be transfusion-dependent the rest of her life. I couldn't imagine this for Mom.

[3]*INR definition.* 2017. URL: http://www.allina-health.org/CCS/doc/Consumer_Lab/49/150398.htm

[4]*Myelofibrosis definition.* 2017. URL: http://www.mayoclinic.org/diseases-conditions/myelofibrosis/basics/definition/CON-20027210

Chapter Five

MOM'S SKILLED NURSING FACILITY EXPERIENCE

March 10, 2013

The two weeks before Mom's death were grueling. After finishing the tests, the hospital couldn't do anything more for her. With much concern, they released her to a skilled nursing facility. That experience was horrible because she needed more care than they offered.

Mom lasted five days there. The staff couldn't do the medication combination that relieved Mom's nausea, so it returned with a vengeance. They didn't offer the care she needed, and the care they did provide was deficient in many ways.

March 11, 2013

When Bub, Cheryl, and I arrived in the morning, an aide had clothed Mom in her roommate's pants, put a sweatshirt on her, and demanded she wear it even though she was hot and sweaty.

I knelt beside Mom in the wheelchair and held her, telling her we would change her right now. Cheryl and Bub went and bought Mom larger pants to deal with her swollen stomach.

Mom did well with the physical therapy she received there. Her ninety-four-year-old sister had instructed her on how to use a walker—

she zoomed down the hall with it, making sure she stood inside of it and not hunched over.

Mom's nausea continued, and we battled with her to eat. She hated eating when she felt nauseous because it caused her to vomit. An aide forced her to eat in the dining hall, and she begged me to eat in her room. When I calmed her and asked why, she cried and said, "I'll vomit," and that's exactly what happened. Embarrassed, she turned her back to the room, and we both whimpered. I cleaned her up. Bub and I took her back to her room and never returned to the dining room.

March 12, 2013

We wrestled with the care she received from the staff: the assigned doctor and the aides. We met with the administrator of the facility to no avail. They did repeat her physical therapy, and she did well. She liked being able to get up and move.

March 13, 2013

When we arrived in the morning, we were horrified at the facility's callous treatment of my mom. Her roommate told us that Mom vomited the night before. "Your mom sat for quite a while with the vomit streaming down the front of her gown. Then when the aid finally did respond to the call, he threw a washcloth at her and said, 'Clean yourself.'"

Her roommate also said Mom screamed "Larry" several times during the night.

I have no idea which Larry she wanted: her nephew Larry Waldroup, possibly. I wondered if Mom didn't feel safe there and was calling out a familiar name to rescue her.

This all compounded my anger. I was furious! Bub and I already had met with the administrator with a list of complaints but to no avail.

❄

Later the physician assigned to Mom verbally attacked me, insisting I was in denial and Mom needed hospice care. Mom was with me and she heard every word and witnessed my distress! I hated that she heard this doctor's rant, my angry response, and the word, "hospice."

I thought, "Mom walks with a walker; she doesn't need hospice." Panic seized my heart—I could feel everything shifting, and I didn't know how to stop it. I couldn't imagine a health care professional dismissing my mom in such a demeaning manner.

I thought a skilled nursing facility would take better care of her, but they provided minimal care when she needed more intensive help. I had no idea that she had slipped that much—I wanted them to provide what she needed, and they either couldn't or wouldn't.

So I stayed with Mom that night to protect her from the staff, sleeping on a mat on the floor. She received better treatment with me there because I demanded it. Bub stayed out in the car and came in often to check on us throughout the night. We all experienced a restless night.

Mom liked me staying the night with her, but she hated me sleeping on the floor. She was so sick. I listened to her restlessness: one minute she was asleep, then she sat up in bed, rolled her shoulders, arched her back, and moaned. The pain in her back was killing her— her swollen spleen crowded all her other organs and hurt.

Late in the evening, Mom, with eyes closed, voiced the following words, and I wrote them out on my iPad. Words have always been important to me and I knew I had to record hers.

MOM'S WORDS TEN DAYS BEFORE SHE DIED

March 13, 2013

Momma, Momma
Help
Please
I am sorry
I told Mom I wanted to be with her.
Larada, I want to be with you!
I don't know what to do.
Please get it done!
I want God!
Wow! (strongest voice I'd heard from her in a couple weeks)
I want this done.
I can't get done.
Larry (repeatedly)

As I wrote these words and phrases down and watched her restlessness, I feared that she was moving in a direction I didn't want her to go, but there was nothing I could do about it.

When she shouted, "Wow!" in the strongest voice I'd heard in weeks, I wondered what or who she was seeing.

March 14, 2013

That morning, Bub and I felt defeated. The skilled nursing facility didn't give the dietary support Mom needed with her swallowing issue. I couldn't stay each night with her to protect her from the night staff. It just didn't work, so we gave in to going to hospice. I worked to get her in the hospice I wanted, but Mom's raging fever returned, so she returned to the hospital that afternoon.

Mom was so sick and she was afraid of the ambulance ride. The drivers let me ride in the back with her and it helped calm her down.

Chapter Six

MOM'S PROGRESSION

Even before going into the skilled nursing facility, eating had become a major issue for Mom. Her swallowing made it difficult—she choked and then vomited; her swollen spleen crowded her other organs and caused severe nausea, and she had no appetite at all. In fact, she refused to eat at all.

March 14, 2013

On her return to the hospital, the ER doctor told my brother and me if Mom didn't eat, they would have to put in a feeding tube. I warned Mom about this, and she cried, "I can't eat, but I don't want to die." And we battled to keep her alive!

She kept slipping because of her refusal to eat, and we could do nothing. I tried everything, but she was so sick.

Mom's floor nurse, Reese, cared for her like she was her own mother. She often said to Bub and me that she so admired how we were taking care of our mother—that so many elderly people go through the end of their life alone.

Bub and I worked as a team in the hospital. He was the good guy; I was the bitch. Often, he roamed the halls, talking to the staff and learning important personal information, then he would relay it to me: "Mary's daughter is sick. Be patient with her today."

My job was to be the hard-nosed bitch—arguing and demanding with the staff to treat my mom with care. This pairing worked well.

Many visits from family and friends blessed Mom during her hospital stays: Rhonda Sandoval, Gerry Dunbar, John Dussart, Jackie Mock, Rose Ward, Carlos Sandoval, Larry Waldroup, Gary and Diane Adams, Jim and Karen Doherty, Cassidy Doherty, Aunt Willie and Janet, Sue, Larraine, Jeff, and Lee-Ann. Each visit uplifted her, and Mom enjoyed the time shared, but she downplayed her illness to everyone except her sister.

March 15, 2013

When Aunt Willie and Janet arrived, Mom grabbed Aunt Willie's hand and hugged her. She cried into her big sister's shoulder, "Oh, Willie, I am so sick!" I had no idea before then that Mom had understood how sick she was.

For some reason, Mom told Aunt Willie and Janet about us eating pizza at our house, so I suggested to Lin that he wear his pizza hat when he came the next day.

Because of Mom's release from the hospital to the skilled nursing facility, the Jakafi order got lost in the shuffle. But now back at the hospital, I tried to order the Jakafi, but the secretary in the oncologist's office focused on the wrong thing—the financial aide; she'd missed that all we needed was Mom's credit card number. We lost two days of medication because of this.

March 16, 2013

Lin came prancing in the door of Mom's hospital room with his famous pizza hat on, and we had a good laugh. When he got ready to leave, Mom wanted to keep the hat, so he left it with her.

March 18, 2013

Twelve days earlier I had filled out the application for Jakafi, the trial drug for myelofibrosis. We decided to try it, hopeful that the drug would be effective. The medical world we dealt with didn't have the same sense of urgency that we did, but I had finally been approved for the drug. We had to get the drug here from Texas, so they overnighted it, but I could see Mom was slipping quickly. She ended up only taking four pills before she passed away. The drug cost $10,000 per month. Out of this amount, we would pay $2,700 per month. We paid one payment hoping to miraculously save her.

At first, the oncologist who diagnosed Mom warned she needed to take it for a month to notice any effect, and another older oncologist confirmed this. The younger oncologist shared on the day Mom passed that it would have taken six months to see any change—she didn't have a month, but she sure didn't have six months!

On the Monday evening before she died, Mom spoke her last words when *Dancing with the Stars* came on the TV.

All excited, I said, "Mom, *Dancing with the Stars* is on. Aren't you excited?" She said in a sarcastic tone, "Oh, yea."

March 19, 2013

The Jakafi arrived at our house at 11:00 A.M., and Lin brought it down to me—$10,000 worth of medication in a small, white jar. I stared at the label, mesmerized by the fact that this little container cost $10,000, and it could save Mom's life. The day started off on the right foot.

Mom's swallowing capability was fading, so the doctor wanted to put in an NG tube so she could take the Jakafi. The tube was supposed to be put in that afternoon. The hospital rule was that the floor nurse and a radiologist had to try to place it in her first in her room upstairs before calling in a specialist.

Mom's platelets were way down, so they wanted to do a platelet transfusion before putting in the tube, and she needed irradiated platelets, so that took longer to get.

They tried to put the NG tube in at 4:30 P.M. and failed. The specialist downstairs had already gone home, so we had to wait until tomorrow. Bub and I knew we were running out of time.

Overwhelmed, I sat quietly beside Mom's bed, bewildered and

defeated. I felt at an all-time low. I wanted to get the NG tube in so we could get Mom on the road to recovery. The food battle had worn us both down. I had to be strong and battle with her to eat; she refused and I insisted. This cycle continued.

A pharmacist from the hospital came in to talk to me about the Jakafi treatment. I sat silent and didn't look at her, fighting back tears.

She gently grabbed my arm and whispered, "Ms. Horner, you taught me English and Spanish in Raton. I'm Jenny Baca Miles."

I grabbed her and hugged her close, sobbing. Not only was she a special student of mine, but she went on an educational trip to Mexico with me in 1990 with three other girls. We caught up on our lives and then we talked about Mom and her treatment. I worried about handing over the expensive Jakafi to her, and Jenny understood my concern, so I gave her four days worth of the medicine. Finally, something went right.

March 20, 2013

Today was Dad's birthday—Bub and I both feared Mom would die on this day, but she kept going.

At 9:00 A.M., Bub and I went with Mom downstairs to have the specialist place the NG tube. We waited forty-five minutes. Mom's nose bled, so the radiologist wanted to stop it, but they called Mom's nurse, Reese, and she said, "No, don't stop!" and came down to help. They had Mom laying down flat, so Reese sat her up, and it worked.

Preparing to leave after that long hard Wednesday, I let Mom know we had to go, and she panicked, repeating, "NO, NO, NO!" and grabbed our hands. It broke our hearts to leave her that night.

We celebrated that day because Mom finally received her first dose of Jakafi—we really believed it would somehow miraculously save her! After all the work of getting the Jakafi here, she only took four tablets.

March 21, 2013

The doctor wanted to put in a PICC line to relieve Mom's swollen and bruised arms from the multiple blood draws and blood transfusions. At this point we had lost count of the blood transfusions, they were so numerous. The PICC line was way too late!

The feeding tube silenced Mom, and she appeared to be resting.

But we had to use an instrument to suction ugly, bloody liquid out of her throat—this was something new.

March 22, 2013

Friday passed with no procedure; the week had been so full and demanding. I had trouble sleeping that night—later Bub shared he did, too.

That afternoon, Mom became listless and non-responsive to the physical therapist who tried to have her move her left leg; her condition worsened rapidly.

Reluctantly at this point, my prayers changed. Reality became more clear, and I started praying for God's mercy and grace instead of begging him for Mom's healing. I had learned this lesson right before Dad died.

March 23, 2013

Bub and I followed our morning routine: rise early and arrive at the hospital by 7:30 A.M.

Overnight Mom had changed drastically. When we arrived, she stared at the ceiling, moaning and wailing. She couldn't talk to us. Dr. Wilson, the rotation doctor assigned to Mom, alerted us that they thought something had happened during the night, and there may be brain damage now. The doctor said we had three choices: continue what we were doing, get an MRI to identify any brain damage, or put her in hospice there at the hospital and let her go.

Tearfully, I called Lin to confer with him. He said to ask the doctor what she would do if it were her mother. I didn't know what else to do.

Bub and I decided to do the MRI, but we wanted to talk to the oncologist. We were fortunate that that particular oncologist was assigned that morning to Mom. In her quiet manner, she informed us that Mom would have to take the Jakafi for six months before we could notice any difference—not a month to six weeks like the two older oncologists had advised. She also gently guided us: if this were her grandmother, she would put her in hospice and love her to the end. God's answer to Lin's question came with this gentle woman's suggestion.

After the oncologist left, Bub walked to one side of Mom's bed and I walked to the other. We released her, saying, "It's time to stop fighting. You can go to Dad and Jesus, and we will be okay." We sobbed; she moaned, eyes fixated on the ceiling.

After we made the decision to move Mom to hospice, the morning filled with family visits: Aunt Joan Doherty, Mark, Dianna, and Zac Fox drove for four and a half hours to see Mom. They circled her bed and tearfully said their goodbyes.

My brother's oldest daughter, Connie, and her three children came from Texas to visit her, too. Lisa, our second cousin, flew in that afternoon to see her favorite Aunty. Loved ones surrounded Mom the whole day.

The option to move her to hospice in the hospital seemed so right —no ambulance ride somewhere else. The doctor feared that she was too weak to be transferred. The staff quietly moved Mom to a private hospice room located on her same floor a little after 3:00 P.M.

I whispered to the hospice nurse, "I have a question," and she knew what it was I needed to know before I asked: "How long could it take?" She said she thought Mom wouldn't last through the night.

We gathered around her bed, loving her and knowing that the end was coming. When the doctor used an instrument to suck the bloody liquid from Mom's throat, I suggested Lisa and Connie leave the room. They both recoiled and left. We had been sucking bloody liquid from her throat all week and didn't even notice how horrible it was anymore.

A nurse brought in a cart with food and drinks. Prior to this, Bub and I had gotten food in the cafeteria, but it ended up under our chairs not touched.

The hospice nurse gave Mom two morphine shots to ease her suffering. She kept moaning and staring at the ceiling.

I witnessed my mom die, standing by her side. My brother, Bub, stood on the other side of the bed with his oldest daughter, Connie, next to him. Our cousin Lisa stood beside Connie. Connie's children chose to wait outside in the waiting room.

I leaned in close to Mom at her right side with Reese, her faithful nurse, beside me.

I played "Amazing Grace" on my iPad—Mom's favorite hymn. I watched the process unfold before me. With my eyes glued to her face, I watched her mouth and her breath, dreading her last one.

Lin lingered in the shadows with Dr. Wilson.

Her breathing changed—longer time between breaths. Her lips turned blue. I stroked the blue veins on the side of her face. It was not just her breath that changed—her skin appeared transparent. Her last breath came and went as I watched.

Dr. Wilson did three tests to see if she was dead: listened to her heart for one full minute, stuck a tissue in her eye to see if she flinched, and pinched her thumb. She was gone.

The universe shook on March 23, 2013 at 5:10 P.M. My world will never be the same.

Bub reached across the bed and grabbed me, sobbing, "Don't blame yourself. We did all we could do. You did so much. There was nothing else to do."

His consoling spirit soothed a part of me that only he could. I had worked so hard to help Mom, to get the Jakafi here, to find the right doctor, the right treatment and in the end, it didn't matter. Bub knew my heart and my desires, thank God!

Throughout this whole ordeal, my God kept popping in and surprising me with moments of His grace, delightful occasions in the midst of chaos to remind me that He was present in all of it. I call those special interventions "God Things" and listed them in Appendix A.

Mom got sick at the beginning of January and died March 23— three short months, but looking back now, I realize she had been sick for months. I also realized God in his infinite grace and mercy took her swiftly.

Chapter Seven

PRIVILEGE OF SERVING MOM AND DAD

For what purpose are we put on this earth, anyway? It can be so confusing sometimes with all the advertisements that say this and that will satisfy my every need.

Familial commitments have changed with many elderly people left to handle the end of their lives alone. Reese, Mom's faithful nurse at the end, often stated how lucky Mom was to have Bub and me there to take care of her. She said many elderly people are on their own at the end of their lives.

My belief is that my primary purpose on this earth is to be of service to others, especially my family. It was an amazing privilege to be of service to my mom and dad, especially in their last days.

Dad's decline was rapid. I helped Mom in those last months of Dad's life with important decisions about his care. Because I lived so close and was single, I could come and support her as needed.

Over the seventeen years after Dad died, I helped Mom—more and more as she aged. I tried to be sensitive and not usurp her power. She was used to living alone, taking care of herself and managing our family ranch until January 15, 2013, just three months before she passed.

How do you do that? How do you help an aging parent without taking away their independence and power? Looking back, I had to walk a fine line in the last few years she was healthy, but Mom was really Miss Independent, and I respected that. We were able to maintain that balance, and she was the primary decision-maker as long as she could be. I treated Mom as an equal, not as a little old lady that needed me or my help.

Early on in Mom's illness, I told her that no decision would ever be made concerning her medical care without her input. I repeated this important commitment many times during her illness and adhered to it until she could no longer contribute.

PRIVILEGE OF WITNESSING MOM'S DEATH

I wasn't present when Dad died, and I have always regretted that. After missing that, I so wanted to be with Mom, and it truly was an honor. There is a definite process to death and after having been there through the death of my friend Kathi Raver in 2009, I could see what was happening. This helped prepare me for Mom's death.

Standing beside someone in death and seeing that last breath come is amazing. My eyes were glued onto Mom's mouth and her labored breath. I watched each breath and watched again and held my own, fearing it was her last one, repeating that again and again. I held my breath until she breathed and then we repeated it. The hospice nurse told us that she would not last long, so I knew it was coming. But how long—two hours? Four?

When it did finally come—the last breath, I was shocked and devastated! Our three-month struggle and battle ended.

We had done everything we could. As sick as she was, I still believed that we would somehow get through this, especially when the oncologists convinced us that Jakafi would make a difference. Denial is a powerful tool of survival. I know that I'm the eternal optimist and that's okay, but it didn't happen.

At the end, Mom was non-responsive. We feared there was brain damage. At this point, blood transfusions kept her alive because her bone marrow wasn't producing any blood. There was no way that I would want her to live that way. In reality, thankfully death came, and God's mercy and grace won again.

Yes, it is a privilege to witness the end of a dear one's life on this earth. It stirred unsettling thoughts in me about what's next. Where is Mom now? Where is Dad? What will my death be like? Who will stand beside me? Will I be alone?

Obviously these questions can't be answered on this side of death, but I faced my own mortality.

Chapter Eight

THE AFTERMATH

March 23, 2013

After Mom died, we stayed with her for a while—I just couldn't leave her. I knew she was gone, that the shell of her worn-out body wasn't her, but it was all I had to hold on to right now. I cried and cried. I circled the room and received hugs from everyone there, but I returned to Mom as though she drew me to her. I touched her wrinkled arthritic hands, the blue vein that stood out on the side of her face. People tried to console me, but it didn't help.

I sat across the room from Mom, trying to take it all in, but again I stood up and walked to her side. Again I had to connect with her. I touched her soft, familiar face, her worn-out hands—a lifeless corpse now. I knew that vivacious, lovely lady was gone.

In a stupor, I called family and friends to let them know—I felt like a robot conveying my sad message. I was in shock and doing what needed to be done. That's what I always do.

It's funny how small specific items become the focus at a time like this. I wanted to make sure that I had Mom's false teeth with me. She had a thing about people seeing her without them. I knew she would be viewed at the funeral home, and she had to have her false teeth.

I queried the nurses about the location of the false teeth; I focused on this driving issue; it was paramount now. I found out they had them and would give them to the ambulance driver who moved Mom's body to the funeral home in Trinidad, Colorado. I relinquished the strong need to personally have them with me.

We finalized details about her transport to Trinidad, and I kept putting off the inevitable—leaving Mom at the hospital. My dear family understood my need to stay, to touch her and to cry, but it was time.

Leaving Mom there alone was one of the hardest things I have ever done in my life. I had to walk away and leave her body there. She had been my sole focus for the last three months, a major focus for the last seventeen years since Dad passed away, my dear friend, my first play-mate, and the woman who carried me! How could I walk away now?

I felt hollow walking through the hallway and diverted my eyes to not make eye contact with any of the dear nursing staff that had cared for Mom. Resolutely, I entered the elevator and solemnly rode down-stairs. My feet felt like concrete blocks as I trekked out of the hospital. When we got outside, the sun blinded me—how could it keep shining?

People passed us, laughing and carrying on like nothing had happened. I barely stopped myself from screaming, "Shut up. My mom died. Please be quiet. Please respect my pain." With Lin on one side of me and Bub on the other, they directed me down the sidewalk to our car.

The three of us drove home in silence, occasionally interrupted by my whimpers. My niece Connie and her three children gathered their belongings at a nearby motel, drove to our house, and spent the night. Our cousin Lisa also joined us for the evening.

It was a tearful, sad evening with my family surrounding me.

Because it was a Saturday night, we watched Mom's favorite country and western shows on RFD-TV. Bub sat by himself in a rocker near me. I sat next to Lin on our love seat. The rest sat on the sofa or on the floor nearby.

A favorite song came up on the TV show, and Bub jumped up sobbing, grabbed me, and directed me to the kitchen where we danced, each of us leaning into each other, sobbing. What a poignant moment that was—our parents raised us to be dancers. So what did we do in our pain? Dance and cry in each other's arms!

I cried myself to sleep that night, with Lin holding me in his arms —a routine that we repeated every night afterwards for months.

March 24, 2013

Waking that first morning without the urgency to go to the hospital shocked me. It had been my routine. I rolled over to Lin, sobbing, and he gathered me in his arms. How would I manage my life now without Mom?

Connie and her children returned to their home in Texas so they could come to Branson, Colorado for Mom's memorial service in a few days.

Friends from Albuquerque brought food and hugs. I spent the day trying to finalize the date of Mom's service. We had a date conflict with a dear family friend from Kim, Colorado whose service was going to be Friday morning, March 29th—the date we wanted to have Mom's service. The second choice would have been Saturday, March 30th, but the cemetery didn't open graves on Saturday, so we had to delay it until Monday, April 1st—our third choice.

Lisa lingered after Connie left, consoling Bub and me with her humorous nature. I asked her to go shopping with me the next day to pick out the outfit Mom would be buried in, and she happily agreed.

I dreaded going to bed that night because in the dark quiet of the night, the pain overcame me in waves. In the quiet solitude, I let down my defenses and cried and cried, and Lin held me.

March 25, 2013

Early that morning as I awoke, I realized I needed to ask Bub to join Lisa and me on our shopping trip. I knocked on his bedroom door, and he ushered me in. I sat down on the edge of the bed and we exchanged small talk, then I asked him, "Do you want to go with Lisa and me today?"

His eyes shone with tears. "Yes, I do." He needed to be a part of this healing activity. Lisa made the whole experience bearable! She has a natural gift for humor at the right time, and we needed it!

March 26, 2013

Bub's son, Andy, flew in from California early afternoon, then the three of us drove to Branson, stopping in Raton, New Mexico to get groceries.

All three of us sat still as we pulled up to Mom's house and stared at her home. A short three months earlier, she had cried when we left, wondering if she would ever return. I hadn't been back there in the interim. I sobbed and sobbed; Bub and Andy helped me inside. I surveyed each room with care, touching items that she had touched.

We had a tasteless dinner and headed to bed.

Washing my face and preparing for bed, I closed the bathroom door —Mom's nightgown hung on a hook behind the door.

I screamed, and Bub and Andy came running. I sobbed uncontrollably and showed it to them. Bub stashed it away in a drawer. After I calmed down, I saw it was missing. I asked him to get it, and I slept with it in my arms that night and many nights afterwards—in fact, it's still under my pillow at home.

I could smell Mom with her gown so close. That familiar aroma comforted me yet broke my heart because I knew it would fade away eventually. Andy wanted to sleep in Mom's bedroom, and I was so glad. I slept in my old familiar bedroom, so overcome with grief, I could hardly stand it.

March 27, 2013

Bub, Andy, and I set up the funeral arrangements sitting around Mom's round table. Andy looked through her paperwork for any clues about her service. In her last days, Bub and I had not talked to Mom about what she wanted because we kept thinking that she would live.

I thumbed through her Bible and found three verses she wanted at her service. I cried with joy.

At this point, like a bolt of lightning, I remembered Mom often repeating my whole life, "When I die, please play 'Stardust' at my funeral."

I contacted her minister about the service and our longtime family friend Sam Bachicha about the songs we wanted him to sing—the plans came together.

With some reservation, I told Bub and Andy that I wanted "The Beer Barrel Polka" played when the family was seated. Bub gasped and shook his head, "No," but later agreed. Mom loved *Molly B's Polka Party* and watched it every Saturday night, polkaing around the living room alone—I knew she would be smiling! We also played a mixture of Big Band music before the service—Mom and Dad danced to many of the big bands.

We decided to use a poem I had written when Mom turned seventy-five as the basis for her eulogy, so all we had to do was tweak it to make it appropriate. I asked several family members to read it and help edit it.

We also decided to read a poem I wrote about Mom, "The Fragrant Lilac of My Life." It was my Christmas gift to her in 2003, and she framed it and had it up on her wall in the living room.

I knew I couldn't read these at the service without sobbing uncontrollably, so Lin read the eulogy and my poem, and he did a heartfelt job.

March 28 – 30, 2013

Over the next couple days, a steady stream of friends brought over delicious food so we wouldn't have to worry about cooking. As they stayed and talked, many shared their favorite stories about Mom, and it was a celebration. I cried in the arms of many of these life-long friends over my loss.

Bub, Andy, and I met with the mortician, Tom Murphy, to finalize the plans and select her casket. We chose a beautiful simple wooden one she would have liked. She often talked about someone in the area who made pine box caskets and how she loved the simplicity, so that guided our choice. We gave Tom the purple nightgown we had bought for Mom on our shopping excursion. We also gave him an afghan we wanted draped over her—it had a photo on it of Mom and me with Bub's family, and she treasured it.

I did what I had to do: plan the service, create the eulogy, be hostess to my family members, and I cried and cried.

Family members arrived to attend Mom's memorial service—all had to drive to Branson because it's hours away from the nearest airport. My nieces and nephew decided where they were going to sleep with their families. We had two full houses—Mom would have been in her glory with everyone there.

March 29, 2013

We all caravanned to the mortuary in Trinidad to view Mom's body. Her lips were not right, so I redrew them before they opened the viewing to the public. My cousin Janet and my niece Cheryl stood by me and supported me as I did this sad task. I was willing to redraw my sister-in-law's lips when she died in 2005, and I knew I could do it for Mom, too.

As I rested my hand on Mom's cold hard chin, I was reminded that this was not my precious mom.

Afterward, different members of the family brought specific items they wanted buried in the casket with her.

March 30, 2013

More neighbors dropped by with food and their condolences.

Connie, Cheryl, and Kendra prepared eggs, baskets, and goodies for their children for Easter the next day—I barely remember any of this!

March 31, 2013

Easter Sunday! All of Bub's children and grandchildren celebrated that special holiday with us at Mom's house the day before her service. It felt so appropriate to think of resurrection after her death—it was comforting.

But such a strange mixture of emotions—I reveled in the opportunity to see my young great-nieces and -nephews search for Easter eggs. Laughter and screams of joy filled the air. I sat on the front porch in Mom's housecoat (I felt her arms around me wearing her clothes) with my coffee cup in hand. Other grown-ups joined me as we watched the Easter tradition continue. But tears streamed down my cheeks as I watched, missing Mom and knowing that tomorrow would be so very hard to endure.

April 1, 2013

The poignancy of Mom's service on April Fools' Day caused me to chuckle—this was a God Thing for sure. For two reasons it was right: Mom's best friend's, Helen Waldroup's, birthday was April 1st, and Mom loved to pull practical jokes on people.

The service was exactly what I wanted to do to honor my dear mom. She didn't want a PowerPoint slideshow of pictures or posters full of photos in the chapel, so we did one picture on the program. We focused on music she loved, and Lin read the eulogy and my poem.

Because I was a middle school teacher, we had a group participation part of the eulogy where people raised their hands if they had . . .

- Eaten a meal prepared by Elva?
- Cooked one of Elva's recipes: Dr. Barglow's wife's pie crust or Pearle Horner's dinner rolls?
- Played a sport where Elva cheered you on?
- Had a prank played on you by Elva?
- Sat around a table at craft club, talking, giggling, and making crafts with Elva?
- Shared a dance floor with Elva and her favorite dance partner, Harold?
- Sat at Elva's round table and played games with her?

At the service I sat nestled and comforted between Lin and Bub—Bub had his arm around me and we folded into each other at heart-wrenching times during the service, both heartbroken, tears gliding down our cheeks.

Lin and I rode in the family limousine to the cemetery with my two sisters and their husbands and Scott Warner, our family friend. When we pulled up to the gaping hole in the ground, I gasped. The thought of Mom buried in the ground overwhelmed me—it took my breath away.

My sister, Larraine, tried to distract me from looking at the grave, but I fixated on it.

The service was short. Family and friends hugged me and shared in my sorrow.

Again, it was hard to leave Mom—like the day Mom died in the hospital. The thoughtful worker at the cemetery knelt and prayed at the edge of Mom's grave—with his shovel beside him. He waited to do anything until we left.

The Branson Community had a dinner for us at the Community Center after the service.

April 6, 2013

After the service, Bub came back to Tijeras, New Mexico with us, and on Saturday, April 6th the three of us went to a George Strait concert that we had bought tickets for a couple months before. We knew Mom would want us to do that.

April 7, 2013

Bub left that afternoon after being away from home for about six weeks. Seeing Bub leave ended this whole insane episode of my life, and I cried in his arms before he boarded the plane.

I had no idea what to do now that it was all over.

Chapter Nine

HOW MY POETRY AND PROCESS HAPPENED

Over the years, recovery taught me the value of writing as a healing tool, so I knew the power of the written word, but my love of poetry came out of my teaching career and my heart.

When I was working on my BA degree in English at Colorado State University, I had to do a ton of writing, mostly essays to fulfill the demands of the degree, and I loved it. We read poetry in my required English classes, and for the first time in my life, it spoke to a deep part of me that I didn't understand.

At this time, I wrote a story that later became my second self-published book, *When Will Papa Get Home?,* and the words flowed. In fact, I spent one summer writing night and day.

In my early teaching career, I dabbled in poetry but nothing serious. I taught a poetry unit every year, and my love for poetry grew as I shared beautiful, meaningful poems with my students.

I had studied the power of writing and started the habit of writing with my students daily in their English classes. I attended the National Writing Project, a professional development plan that encouraged lots of writing and deemed myself a writer!

From the National Writing Project, I wrote another book that later became my first self-published book, *This Tumbleweed Landed.* Originally it was a collection of poetry that chronicled my childhood growing up in a small ranching community during the fifties and sixties, but I added stories about my ranching experiences and expanded the reach of the book.

At this point in my life, I didn't see poetry as a healing tool—I saw it as a meaningful means of communication. I wrote poems about important dates and people and loved how it felt and worked. I played with it and began seeing myself as a poet.

Over the years, I attended several poetry classes put on by Continuing Education, dabbling in different forms and continued to be drawn to free verse—rhyming poetry didn't work for me.

After the end of my third marriage, I wrote volumes of poetry and learned that it was a wonderful tool to heal a broken heart.

Before Mom died, I wasn't writing regularly. In 2011, I wrote a poem for Lin that I read to him at our wedding. Several people came up to me after I read it, saying that they didn't know that I was a poet. That really bothered me—I had let my writing go once again.

For the first seven weeks after Mom died, I struggled with returning to work and living. My health and stomach issues took all my energy, then something changed.

The poetry flowed out of me, first a slow methodical drip, drip, drip, but it gained momentum. I wrote the poetry as a way to process what had happened in those three short months of Mom's decline. Every word I wrote bathed me with a healing calm. The topic of the poem would come to me, and the words poured out of my heart onto the page. The poems are not in chronological order of when the topic occurred but in the order they came.

❄

How do you handle grief?

My parents showed me how they handled the loss of their parents. Each had a different process but they mourned, they grieved, they had a process.

My mom's example of how she handled her grief when my dad died spoke deeply to my heart. Her mood swings were palatable. She would be totally okay, then she would slip into her grief and scream and cry. Every ounce of her small body was grieving, and then she would be okay again. She did this cycle for years, and she dealt with her anger.

Her advice to anyone about grief was "grieve your own way." We all grieve differently, and that was what gave me permission to do it my way. Writing poetry became the cornerstone of how I moved through the grief and the loss.

The original title for this book and my triumphant poem it's named after came to me very soon after losing Mom. "I Grew Up to Be the Woman I Always Wanted To Be" resonated with me, because in the midst of the loss and pain, a deep peace settled in my heart at different times. I had passed the test; I had stood strong in the midst of adversity and chaos. I was proud of how I had handled Mom's sickness and death.

The next chapter is my poetry, starting on May 11, 2013 and ending May 26, 2017. If you are someone who doesn't normally read poetry, take a breath, listen to the feelings that are expressed in the words of my poems and see if they resonate with some feeling deep inside. You don't have to understand the poem—look for the feeling of the poem and how it connects for you. Hopefully the words that healed me will help you on your path of grief!

Chapter Ten

MY HEALING POETIC JOURNEY AND MY PROCESS

My poems are not in the order they occurred—they are mostly in the order I wrote them. It's fascinating to me what mattered deeply for me at different times and how the memories and topics came in random order.

I added the last few poems when I realized that I had not addressed some priceless topics.

NO WORDS NOW

May 11, 2013

Mom died March 23, 2013
   No words
   No poems
   until May 2.

Lost in the pain
   drowning
   suffocating
   Words frozen
   gone
   void

All I had was pain!
   Loud
   screeching
   screaming pain.

Normally, poetry is my respite
    My sanctuary
    I visit to
    understand this world

Nothing there!
    Only the deep, dark hole
    The consuming loss
    The utter defeat

Missing Mom
    and
    trying to live!

THE GRIEF IS OVERWHELMING

May 2, 2013

Mom died on that fateful day.
    A part of me died, too!

The grief is overwhelming,
    My nerves are raw!
    Touch me and I will shatter
    And break into
    Numerous bloody pieces!

The immediate days afterwards blur
    before me
    into one long sob!

The week before her death
    I can recall day
    by day

minute by minute
The exactness of the horror and fear
resonate in my bones and soul.

We had gotten the drug
    Jakafi
    after work, fear, exertion.
    We stood there
    at the goal line.
    All she needed was
    that magic pill
    and she would be okay.

Wednesday
    The wait for the NG feeding tube
    the first attempt yesterday did not work.

Downstairs to radiology
    The technicians couldn't place the feeding tube,
    so Reese, Mom's floor nurse,
    was called to insert the tube,
    and it worked.

Activity
    Inserting a PICC line
    so no more IVs or
    taking blood
    Necessary
    because of her
    bruised and swollen arms.

Mom didn't want us to leave.

It's Dad's birthday
    Bub and I both feared
    she would die that day
    to be with Dad!
    But she didn't!

Thursday morning
    Could we see a difference?
    No.
    Yes.

Any evidence that Jakafi was working?
    Yes.
    No.

She couldn't move her legs
    in physical therapy
    Stumps
    No movement
    disconnected from instruction.

What appeared to be
    resting
    Some coughing
    Silence—no words.

Bub and I could not sleep Friday night.
    Why?
    Subconscious apprehension?

We could see her worsening
    Before our eyes
    need to suction her mouth
    a bloody mess.

No words
    Quiet
    Foreboding!

Then Saturday
    What a change!

Mom's eyes riveted wide open
    staring at the ceiling
    A fearful expression
    on her face
    I knew
    something had happened
    overnight.

Bub and I prayed the prayer of release
    by her bedside
    that morning
    She died at 5:10 in the afternoon.

I saw her last breath!
    I knew it!
    I felt it
    at the pit of my heart and
    Soul.
    I stopped breathing, too!

SHATTERED HEART AND HOPE

May 2, 2013

At 5:10 P.M.
    My heart and hope shattered
    against the
    closed door of death.

I witnessed death
    saw the process
    wanted to soothe Mom's spirit.

Still she was my first concern
    soft, gentle Christian music she loved
    Played "Amazing Grace."

She wailed
    Yes, it was a wail
    Not from pain, not a cry

A wail.

I witnessed love
    in action
    84 years of loving won
    She was surrounded
    at her last breath
    by love
    Bub
    Me
    Lin
    Connie
    Lisa
    Reese
    Dr. Wilson

Earlier in the day
    Aunt Joan
    Mark
    Dianna
    Zack
    Emmily
    Caden
    Kaylea Raye

Earlier that week
    Aunt Willie
    Janet
    Jim
    Karen
    Sue
    Larraine
    Jeff
    Lee-Ann

Gary
Dianne

84 years of giving
    came to an end
    by total receiving.

During her illness,
    Mom let Bub and me
    wipe her butt
    feed her
    move her
    caress her
    laugh with her
    love her

At her death bed,
    She was encircled with love.

It was a privilege!

MOM'S LIPS

May 2, 2013

Mom's lips were wrong!

In 2005, Lela's lips were wrong!
    Total mistakes

Does death do something
    to lips?

Mom laid in her
    wooden casket
    dressed in purple
    and adorned with a
    family blanket.

With my hand shaking,

I redrew her lips,
with her favorite mauve color,
Janet and Cheryl stood beside me
for strength and support.

My hand rested upon her cold chin,
 Hard and lifeless.

She painted my lips
 when I was a child
 Bright red lips
 Big lips
 Clown lips
 My playful Mom
 my playmate.

Reverently I drew
 her lips
 for the last time
 I studied her familiar face
 her features
 now lifeless
 I touched her cheek
 her arm
 the blue vein near her eye.

I could do this, I knew I could,
 and I did!

WHAT WORDS CAPTURE MY LOSS?

June 19, 2013

What words capture
    my loss?
    Mom—dead!
    Two small words—
    Two words that shouldn't
    be spoken together

My world altered forever!
    I cry!
    I live!
    I cry!

Will the tears end?

Will the pain stop?

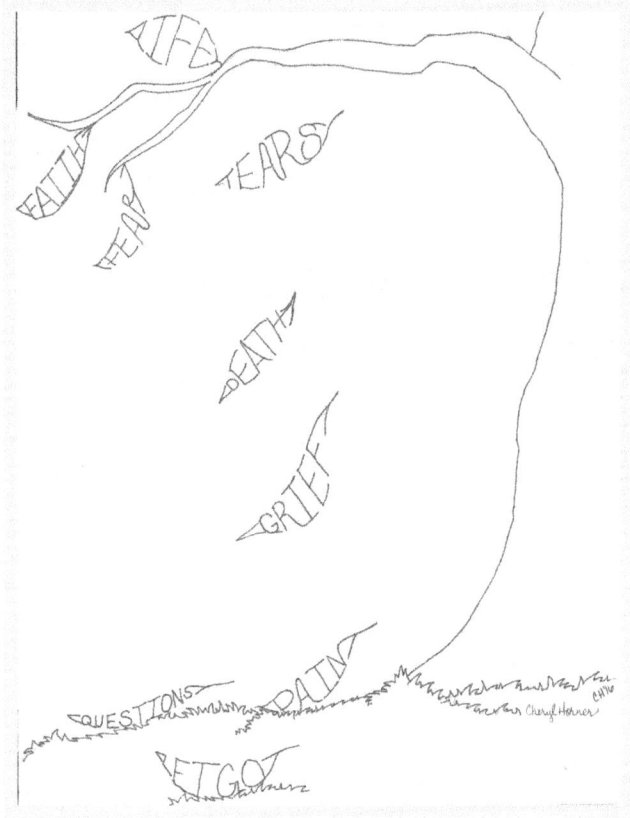

Where are you?
    How are you?

I so need to talk to you
    to touch you
    to hear your voice
    Once again.

Never again!

LIME GREEN

June 19, 2013

You introduced me
    to this color: lime green,
    a favorite of yours for years.
    A tank top for my birthday
    many years ago!

I had never bought it,
    never even considered it.

You did!
    You ventured
    into uncharted areas
    of fashion and style
    for me!

You added something

outrageous
every year to
my wardrobe!

People thought
it was me,
but it was you!

Daring,
innovative
because you knew me.
You knew I'd wear it and
look good.

ARRIVING HOME THE FIRST TIME

July 12, 2013

Any time when I drove up
    in front of Mom's house,
    she bound out the front door
    ecstatic to see me!

"Pulling me down the road!"

Dad did it, too,
    before he died.
    "I pulled you
    down the road,"
    He would say.
    The laughter in his eyes
    reinforced
    the power he thought he had!

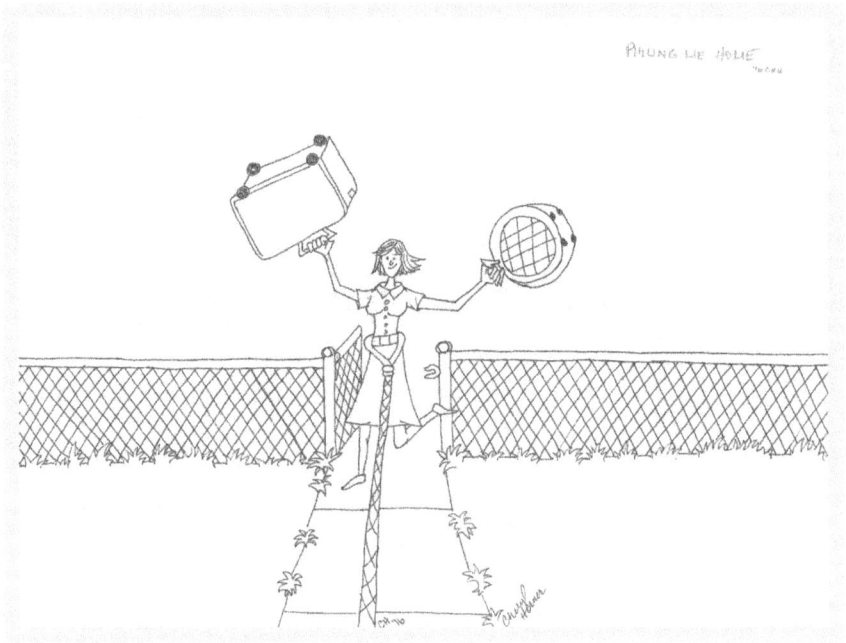

I witnessed Mom
    when I was there once
    waiting for the arrival of
    a family member.

Pacing the floor,
    looking out the front window
    clasping her hands
    looking at the clock
    Waiting!

I knew her routine
    I knew her anticipation
    her joy in my arrival
    and the power in her desire
    for me to come and visit

But she's gone!
    Today I arrive at her home
    with my brother and nephew
    for the first time.

I sit in my car,
    eyes riveted on the front door
    and wait for that familiar figure
    to come bounding out of the house,
    but she doesn't,
    and I cry!

My brother cries
    and touches my shoulder
    He understands the pain

No door opens.
    Mom doesn't greet me
    anymore!

Seeing the joy
    in her eyes
    the hug to her heart
    the help getting my bags
    Inside.

Gone

and I cry!

LUNCH IN THE CEMETERY

July 18, 2013
At Mom's and Dad's Graves

Today I sit in the car
    with my hamburger
    drink
    cookies
    having lunch with Mom
    and Dad!

I sob
    I eat.
    I sob!
    I talk!

Mom did this with Dad
    when he died.
    She told me about her ritual;
    I like it,

so here I am!
I made it mine.

I know she's not here!
    Her body rests here.
    This is where I am
    physically close to her!
    But she's not here.

I speak words for awhile,
    then I just sob,
    Unspoken words
    of my broken heart.

There's solace here
    Peace
    Assurance

My God has always given
    those to me!

I can't hear her voice
    anymore!
    But I still feel her presence,
    her tug on my heart!

After time at their headstone,
I slide in the driver's seat.
The summer breeze blows softly
through the two open windows
on each side of the car.
The rhythmic hiss of the sprinkler comforts me!

Clear blue Colorado sky
    overhead
    with puffy storm clouds
    hanging above the mesa
    named Simpson's Rest,
    a historical site above

Trinidad.

It's a beautiful July day
　　with Mom!
　　The sun warms my bare leg.

Mom bought me this outfit
　　I wear
　　two years ago for
　　my birthday.

I don't care how
　　you grieve!
　　Don't criticize me
　　for how I do!

I have to retell the story
　　over and over again!

I have to say,
　　"I can't believe she's gone"
　　100 x 100 x 100 x100
　　before it will sink in!

I sleep in her bed now in her home,
　　but I can't believe it!
　　I clean her house now,
　　but I ache for her to do it!
　　I write her checks now,
　　but I want to see her signature!

Lunch helps
    at her grave
    with her and Dad
    Breaking bread together
    one more time!

DEATH IS MESSY

August 8, 2013

I knew it was coming,
    deep down in my heart!
    My soul could smell it.
    My spirit could taste
    its sour tang.

I tried to outrun it,
    outsmart it.
    I worked harder,
    I prayed harder,
    Did everything harder.

I held on
    but death won!

Messy and bloody,

but I ignored it!
The stench crept up
slowly out of the corners
of Mom's sterile hospital room.
The lifeless, disgusting odor filled
my nostrils—
But I couldn't identify it
because I wasn't breathing!

I held my breath
    for three months
    her ninety days of decline.
    That way I could control
    the situation
    me
    the inevitable.

I cringed in the reality.

Death softly touched
    my shoulder
    my cheek
    my heart
    but I flinched
    and
    turned away—
    No, ran away!

I refused its grip
    because now it wasn't soft.
    It was brutal,
    bruised fingerprints
    on my arm

from holding on too tight
for days!
It wouldn't let go!

I dug my nails in deeper!
I tried to hold on, Mom,
but you were no longer here
totally.

You had one foot over there!
I didn't realize it,
but you were already gone!

THE MOTHER-DAUGHTER CHAIN

October 14, 2013
Lunch with Dad and Mom

I wanted you to stay
   with me!
   Part of you wanted to stay, too!

My grandma, your mother, beckoned you
   to come!
   Part of you wanted to go!

It was a sacred, otherworldly tug-of-war!

I witnessed your battle
   that Wednesday night at
   the skilled nursing facility

I tried to sleep on the floor,
    but your verbal turmoil kept me
    awake all night!

Ten days before your death
    you wrestled with the
    dilemma:

Go to your Mom, my grandmother
    or
    stay with your daughter, me!

Grandma won;
    I lost!

But someday
    you will win.
    You will tug on
    my heart
    pulling me home
    to be with you!

I have no daughter
    for you to battle with
    on that day.

The Mother-Daughter connection runs
    deep
    timeless
    beyond reality.

Daughter-Mother connection:
  as real as it gets.

SITTING AT YOUR GRAVE—SIX MONTHS LATER

October 14, 2013
Lunch with Dad and Mom

Who am I today?
    Six and a half months
    without you

I miss
    your giggle
    our morning talks
    your advice
    care
    concern
    pride in me
    My eternal cheerleader

I miss
    your familiar smell
    bouncing my life off of you

your stubbornness
determination
Independence

I miss
future fun-filled possible trips
to unknown sights
talks about the Broncos
or Giants

Are we going to win again this year?
a jitterbug with you
trying to recapture
Dad's unique step

I miss you, Mom!

THE HOLIDAYS—I CAN'T

October 14, 2013
Lunch With Dad and Mom

You were my holidays
    for fifty-nine years!

Such a celebrator
    Now I ache
    For your giving spirit!

I face the full holiday season,
    October through January.

I can't do it
    Halloween
    Thanksgiving
    Christmas
    New Year's Eve

Why would I celebrate now?
    For what reason?
    How can I?

My holiday reverberated off of you—
    you made it fun
    authentic!

There was laughter, hugs, smiles, traditions!
    We honored each other.
    We celebrated each other!

Who will buy my special Advent gifts?
    You started this tradition in 1988,
    When I went to treatment,
    and we kept it going all these 25 years.
    Small, silly, inexpensive notions.

Who will I buy an outfit to be alike?
    Dad started this tradition before he passed—
    a Christmas outfit alike for many years
    and we continued it after he died,
    those seventeen years.
    Last year's was a turquoise outfit.

Who will make the gravy for our holiday dinner?
    Who will argue with Aunt Willie about the gravy's
    base?
    Milk or water?
    Who will I watch Jay Leno with

and reminisce about seeing him
finally in Las Vegas, Nevada?

Who will buy the chocolate-covered
cherries for your Branson friends?

This is big!
I have to cry!

WAS I THE DAUGHTER I SHOULD HAVE BEEN?

October 29, 2013

"You're my baby girl forever!"
    A giggle followed that statement
    each and every time
    and
    a sideways glance at me
    for my reaction

You loved to tell me
    that, even
    until I was fifty-nine!
    It was your affirmation,
    your seal of
    approval!

Did I do enough?
    Did I shelter you

from the raging storm?
The doctors
The nurses
The test
The needles
The pain

I asked you if
    you were afraid
    when they put the stint in
    so you could stop the Coumadin.
    You said a resounding, "No!"
    That shocked me—
    I was!

I asked, "Why not?"
    Your sweet answer soothed my soul,
    "Because you are here!"

Did I touch you
    that deeply?

I've always wanted
    to protect you
    from angry words
    from disdain
    from your fears after Dad's death
    from the responsibilities

from living alone
    after being married for 43 years
    from growing older and aging

I tried, Mom,
    did I do enough?

Did I care enough?
    call you enough?
    laugh with you enough?
    spend time with you enough?

My selfish needs took
    me away
    often—
    but you were always
    in my heart.

Did I give you enough
    of me
    of we?

I gave you a shot of Coumadin
    in your tummy.
    I wiped your butt,
    feeling that horrible hemorrhoid!
    I suctioned the bloody mess out
    of your throat.
    I swabbed your bloody mouth.
    I held your hand and whispered
    in your ear during
    the bone marrow biopsy.
    I forced you to eat
    those last few weeks,
    believing I could keep you alive

if you ate.
I worked my magic to get
the Jakafi here to
save you,
but it didn't!

"Did I Do enough?"

Did I do enough?

I GREW UP TO BE THE WOMAN

I Always Wanted to Be

October 29, 2013

I tripped my way through life
    faltering
    failing
    succeeding
    hurting!

I learned how to be
    how to serve
    how to survive

I endured multiple losses
    Granddad and Grandma Horner
    Granddad and Grandma Dickerson
    Dad
    Lela
    Linda

Candy
Kathi
Uncle Hughie
Reu
Helen
Uncle Tanky

I knew someday Mom would
    be added to this list
    but not now!
    I wasn't ready!

Her progression to death's door
    moved quickly.

I garnered all my skills
    my abilities
    my wisdom
    and took control
    took care of her.

I watched my actions
    in the midst of insane chaos
    aware that I took the lead
    in her care.

For two months,
    I was sane
    peaceful
    powerful
    focused
    in the midst of the unknown

and mayhem.
Then one night,
I crumbled
on the dark drive home.

During these two months,
    Lin, Bub, and I conferred
    each night
    long distance
    my brother lives in northern California
    planned together
    supported each other

That overwhelming night I hit a wall;
    I knew I needed more.
    Bub offered to come and help.
    I cried, "Yes, come! I need you."

We shared Mom's last days—
    her two loving children!

Surrounding her with
    our love
    attention
    hugs and kisses
    sweet words
    laughter
    memories

That last fateful day,
    Mom stared at the ceiling.
    She wailed.

Mom couldn't answer a question.
She wailed.
Mom didn't seem in pain,
just vacant
moving on to another world!

Bub and I prayed
   —with tears!—
   release for her
   our mom
   surrender
   let go!

At the end, Bub was on one side of her bed
   me on the other!
   Other family members and hospital staff
   joined us.
   She left us
   and this world,
   wrapped in our love.

Most of the funeral plans fell on my
   shoulders
   as organizer,
   but we collaborated,
   ideas from many family members
   and friends.
   We gave Mom an "Elva Horner"
   send off!

I had a solid knowing,
   a deep satisfaction with myself
   and how I handled her death.

I grew up to be
    the woman I always
    wanted to be
    at fifty-nine years old!

I stayed
    I persevered
    I collaborated
    I sobbed
    I screamed!

At a time I desperately needed it,
    God's grace abounded.

I gave all that I had
    to the woman
    who gave me
    life!

I realized
    that my mission
    in this life
    was complete!

All my other successes
    faded into obscurity!
    All my joys, my triumphs
    meant nothing
    were hollow!
    I knew that I had succeeded

finally by how I handled my
Mom's life and death!

I truly grew up to be the woman I always wanted to be—
   in her passing,
     my mom showed me that truth.

THANKSGIVING BECKONS

November 4, 2013

For many years
    I wasn't present
    with Mom
    at Thanksgiving
    after Dad died!

My ex-husband, Ted, and I danced
    in Dallas,
    My favorite round dance
    festival of the whole year—
    Holiday Hoedown!
    We danced Monday through Saturday
    Rounds teaches and dances
    A square dance on Thanksgiving night
    With a club we loved.

During this time, she was alone!

Mom woke up alone,
no one to greet!
She went to Janet's
but Mom was alone
and
never said a word.

After twelve years,
    Ted and I ended!
    Then it was Mom and me!
    We shared the holiday
    with Candy and Michael
    with Aunt Willie and the Bergs

Lin came into my life and
    we shared it with her
    with Connie and the kids
    with Sue and Fred

Precious holidays where we celebrated
    our family and Mom

Thanksgiving beckons me
    this year
    to be grateful
    in the midst of grief!

I've lost my mom;
    I can give out
    of that loss!

I can serve
    for Mom!

Thanksgiving beckons!
    2013

Lin and me
    quiet
    soft
    gentle
    fun

Mom will be there!
    I will feel her touch
    smell her fragrance
    see her out of the
    corner of my eye!

Mom will be there
    because
    I am there!

THE NIGHT MOM DIED

November 15, 2013

Shock filled my heart.
    My mom died
    at 5:10 P.M.
    on a late sunny Saturday afternoon.

The thought of leaving her lifeless body
    at the hospital ripped
    my heart open!
    I knew once I left, she would be gone.

Mom had been
    my focus
    for three months,
    for seventeen years
    since Dad died,
    for my whole life.

After a lengthy time
    of tears,
    Touching Mom,
    needing to be close to
    her body,
    we left.

We went home
    my brother, silent and hurting,
    another major woman loss for him.
    We buried his wife
    eight years earlier.
    my niece and her family
    my second cousin
    my husband
    sat somber and in shock

We watched mindless TV
    crying
    mourning
    silent yet joined by our broken hearts.

I arranged Mom's transport
    to Trinidad, Colorado
    from Albuquerque, New Mexico,
    about 250 miles.
    God made the arrangements though.
    One of Mom's dear friends
    would be driving the ambulance.

Immediately I had to be
    responsible
    take charge

move forward

A classic country-western
    song came on the TV.
    My brother, sobbing, grabbed me,
    moved me to our kitchen
    and we danced.

We danced and danced
and
cried and cried!
Broken-hearted
our world destroyed,
but we danced!
Snuggled close
his tears mixed
with mine!
Our sweet smells mingled,
dancing to the beat of the drum,
The beat of our broken hearts
We needed our arms
around each other
our hearts touching.
We needed dance!

That's what the Horners do!

WATER OR MILK

November 28, 2013
Thanksgiving Day

Two sisters grew up
    in the same house
    taught and
    mentored by the same
    mother

Both sisters
    remember the required liquid for turkey gravy
    differently

My mom said,
    "Add milk!"

My aunt said,
    "Add water!"

Or was it the other way around.

Neither wrong
    both work!

But one said
    Mother taught me
    Add water.
    The other said
    Mother taught me
    Add milk!

Over the many years,
    lots of teasing
    between these two elderly siblings
    insisting she was right!

Christmas 2012
    My aunt at 92
    My mom at 83
    made gravy together again,
    and the battle began again!

My husband turned
    the corner
    from the bedroom,
    just in time
    to see
    these two posed
    in the kitchen

fists clenched
postured to fight!

The question had come up again!
Facing off—
two older sisters
nose to nose
enjoying
this age old question
one more time!

The winner?
All of us present
who witnessed
the love and joy these
two sisters shared!
And the gravy tasted great!

Was it water or milk?

FIRST THANKSGIVING WITHOUT MOM

November 28, 2013

Experience teaches.
    The first year is often
    hard after a significant loss!

I have dreaded Thanksgiving
    for months!

How do I do it?
    without Mom?
    without her homemade cranberry sauce?
    without her delicious homemade pumpkin and pecan pies?
    without her joyful
    participation in the games?

Breath sucked out

of my lungs!
A gasp
A wail
Endless tears!

But I did it!

I listened
to my needs.
I called family,
and
I cried.

In the morning, I attended a recovery meeting
And shared my pain.
I ate lunch with
my husband.
Leisurely
Delightful

At the
High Noon Saloon and Restaurant
in Old Town Albuquerque,
the same place
we shared
with Mom
three years before
in 2010!

I sat at the table
across from Lin.

Mom whispered in my ear.

I saw her flitter across
    the room.
    She sat on my heart,
    my beautiful wrap
    draped over my shoulders.

She was there—
    physically
    spiritually
    I heard her say
    "Great soup
    Carrot and coriander
    Delicious cranberry sauce
    Spicy sweet potato
    Small piece of pecan pie."

Her pieces of pie were never small!

Her giggle resounded
    in my ears!
    Her twinkly, clear blue eyes
    danced!

She enjoyed the place
    the dinner
    the company
    the atmosphere!

And so did I.

She was there.

Afterwards, it was football games
    And another recovery meeting for me.
    I needed to "bookend" my day
    With stability.

SPACE BETWEEN

November 29, 2013

Thanksgiving
    Christmas
    the space between
    Days
    Weeks

Joyous
    celebration
    preparation

This year
    those empty days
    sucked the life
    out of me!

No Mom

to call
and celebrate
that we put up our festive tree!

No Mom
    to buy
    special ten Advent gifts for
    and relish her response
    to each one of them.

I usually fill
    this space
    with writing out Christmas cards and
    Creating my annual Christmas letter
    And
    Creating my annual calendars as a family gift
    with pictures from the previous year
    decorations
    parties
    shopping
    baking

This year
    What do I do?
    How do I do it?

I solemnly
    go through
    the motions!

I do what
    is expected.

I move mechanically
through the form!

When in reality, I cry.
   I hide.
   I try to remember
   to breathe.
   I isolate!

The miracle of Christmas is
   the Christ Child
   My God
   caring so deeply
   for me,
   that his form
   changed
   so I could touch Him,
   so I could touch Him
   So I could hold Him
   So He could hold me!

My mom is gone!
   I can't change that.
   I can celebrate
   a solitary way
   with my Jesus
   alone!

Because in reality,
   that's how I've grieved—
   alone with Jesus!

IS IT GOOD TO GRIEVE ALONE?

November 29, 2013

I cry every morning
    alone
    the pain that
    breaks my heart—
    my loss of Mom!

It's easy!
    A safe place
    alone with
    my cat, Jesse,
    and my Jesus!
    I cry, I sob, I wail! I moan!

But my grief is not easy
    with others!

My throat constricts
    with my sorrow
    when I look someone else
    in the eyes.
    My words flow
    but not the tears!
    They are stuck
    In the depth of my soul.

I've always been
    social.
    Why is this so hard?

My pain is so big
    so monstrous
    so profound
    It's hard to share!

How do I put into words
    with tears
    the ache?
    the disaster?
    the loneliness?

I hold my breath.

The tears don't come easily
    with others, but
    They do alone
    with my cat
    and my Jesus.

GRAVY FOR CHRISTMAS WITHOUT MOM

December 16, 2013

For an early Christmas
    party and dance,
    I made turkey gravy
    with your help, Mom!

In your absence
    I remembered
    your method
    your care
    your procedure,
    and I tried it!

I was prepared
    for disaster.
    Over the years, I haven't cooked that
    much.
    You were the cook;

you spoiled me!

For many years,
    you did it all!
    Now you're gone,
    and
    I have stepped up!
    I watched you,
    tucked those
    instructive memories away deep!

Last Thanksgiving,
    I called you
    several times.
    My task—
    to bake pies
    for our family gathering.

You laughed;
    We laughed!
    You instructed.
    The pies tasted delicious!

I stand on that memory
    this year!

This year, I cook
    as Elva Horner's daughter,
    And your gravy tasted fine!

MY WAILING

December 16, 2013

In my quiet time
    each morning
    I wail—
    the sound of my voice
    echoes through
    the canyons of my loss!
    It sounds foreign
    strange
    but strong!

I am shocked by the sound
    by the depth.

My grief is strong!
    When I wail,
    it consumes
    my whole body!

Some simple words escape—
"Momma"
but mostly unidentifiable sounds
aching, desperate sounds.

Prayer to my God
    Connection to my loss
    Embodiment of the
    continued sound
    that vibrates in
    my ears.
    Low-pitched
    rumbling, coursing through my veins

At this time
    listening to my pain,
    I comfort me.
    I allow it
    to happen
    I cherish
    these moments!

Because
    I cherish my loss!
    My mom!

The little girl inside me makes
    her strong statement
    in that wail,
    in that word,
    Momma,
    and I can live!

DO I LIVE OR DIE?

December 16, 2013

Mom died and
    a part of me, too!

I wanted to die.
    How do I survive
    without her?

Then a stomach
    ailment hit.
    Mysterious
    painful
    loss of appetite
    Severe weight loss
    Seeing a sad, desolate space
    in my eyes!
    My reflection haunted me—
    a walking corpse!

The thought came repeatedly—
    I could die!
    That would be easy!
    I could do it!

I hid it!
    I told no one of
    these thoughts

A kernel of truth
    my truth, my desire
    I had a choice.

It incubated,
    grew with the uncertainty of
    the source of my pain.

Then a yoga instructor
    said to me over the phone,
    "You can choose to live!"

How did she know?
    Did she hear it in my voice?

Did the desperation
    escape
    ever so slightly through my cadence
    and she heard it.

DO I LIVE OR DIE?

"You can live!"
    A choice!
    No
    Yes
    Maybe

Without Mom?

For Mom!

To continue
    her presence here
    To honor her
    To protect my world
    Yes, I will!
    For Mom and me!

I CAN'T BE YOU!

December 16, 2013

The holidays are here!
    You are the holidays!

I've worked to keep
    you here,
      but you're gone!

I can't be you!
    You were "the cook!"
    I'm not "the cook!"
    I am me,
    but I can bake pies.
    It connects me
    to you!

I will roll out the dough

gently
with your hands
on top of mine.
I will honor Dr. Barglow's wife
with your German pie dough recipe.
I will kiss your cheek
with my tears.
I will mix my sweet tears
with the pumpkin
the pecans
the raisins and coconut

It will be
    ceremonial
    ritual
    holy

Your hands on mine
    small
    arthritic
    liver spots
    rings shining

I will savor
    the time
    the experience
    Your presence
    as I continue
    our heritage.

I am not you!
    I can't be!

I CAN'T BE YOU!

But I can be
    your daughter,
    the continuation
    of you
    the light
    that's you
    the family hub that holds
    it all together!

CHRISTMAS CAME;

I Was Surprised!

December 31, 2013

It's over finally,
    My first without you!

I cried!
    I gave gifts
    I received
    I laughed

I cried more!

Mom, you were there!
    We were in your home!
    A decision I made
    early on!

Lin and me!

It was supposed to be
    with Aunt Willie, too,
    but she couldn't.

So it was
    Lin and me,
    and it was good!

I saw you
    everywhere!

We set up your
    favorite silver retro tree
    purple bulbs
    Totally you!

Then we strung white lights
    around the room
    Something new
    different

I set up a Santa light
    in the picture window
    like you did so many years!

Then Connie and her family came.
    Sad at times
    Joyful at others.

CHRISTMAS CAME;

The house overflowed with
    Our family
    And you.

You were everywhere,
    and it comforted me!

The familiar
    My childhood
    You
    Dad
    Bub
    Granddad Dickerson
    Grandma Dickerson

You were there;
    precious memories abound!

MOM'S LAST NIGHT GOWN

December 31, 2013

Bub, Andy, and I were at
    Mom's house
       three days after her death.

I spied it on
    the hook
       behind the door
       in her bathroom

The air was sucked out of me!
    I sobbed!

She wore it
  the last time she slept here.

She planned to wear
it again
when she returned home!

Bub hid it
in a drawer
to protect me
from remembering
and hurting,
but I found it.

And I slept with it!

From that night on
I cuddled it close to my heart—
a salve to soothe me
near my nose
to smell her
one more time!

Her familiar scent crossed over
from where she is now
to here!

At first nights were hard!
That gown circled
my pain
held me tight
and I could smell her!

It's months later.

Now I sleep with
the gown under
my pillow
every night!

The smell is gone!
But when I go to bed
each night,
it comforts me
anew
again

Mom's last night gown,
a sweet reminder!

STRENGTH IN SURVIVAL

January 2, 2014

Mom died late March 2013
    and I started
    dreading the holidays immediately!

They were months away,
    but my wounded heart knew
    they would be empty
    without Mom.

We've spent so many together
    Thanksgiving
    Christmas
    New Year's Eve

Traditions
    that echo back generations!

Mom celebrated each holiday
    with passion and fire.

Every Halloween,
    she prepared small bags of candy
    and thrilled at each child
    who came to
    "Trick or Treat."

At Thanksgiving,
    The full fare:
    Turkey, dressing, homemade
    cranberry sauce, pies galore,
    and, of course,
    That traditional gravy.

At Christmas,
    Popcorn balls, fudge, more pies
    for my lifetime,
    recipes shared
    Our look-alike outfits
    Advent gifts
    between my mom and me for 25 years

Thanksgiving 2013
    quiet
    Lin and me
    self care
    I made it—
    I survived!

Christmas 2013
    changed plans
    at the last minute
    a service holiday
    so different from our tradition

Christmas Eve church service
    at Mom's church
    Afterwards
    a drive up to
    celebrate with
    my dad's sister, Aunt Joan, and her family,
    Time with her is reminiscent of Dad.

Christmas dinner
    at Denny's
    in Pueblo
    After a cherished afternoon
    with Mom's sister, Aunt Willie.
    Any time with her is still time with Mom.

Time with my niece and family
    ranch time
    wandering around our favorite places
    a mountain lion sighting—maybe
    Then games around Mom's
    round table
    with laughter and fun!

Big celebration
    with Mom's family
    tears all the way home
    gifts commemorating Mom.

Mom present in all the gifts.

New Year's Eve
    dancing in my love's arms
    trying not to remember
    last year with Mom
    in Trinidad.

I'm done!
    I survived!
    I didn't explode
    Nor implode!

I faced it!
    I felt it!
    I cried and cried!

Out of that decision
    I survived
    strength covered
    me like a veil
    with my mother's arms
    around me!

I feel it today!
    I feel the pain.
    I feel the strength!
    I survived!

I DID MORE THAN SURVIVE CHRISTMAS

January 2, 2014

I didn't clench my fist
    or white knuckle it!

I celebrated Mom.
    I created family photo gifts of
    calendars
    pillows
    pillowcases

She was my focus,
    and it helped!

The spirit of giving
    enveloped me!

I gave
  and gave,
  and it all fed me.

It gave me the power
  to do more
  than survive!

I cried deeply
  but also laughed deeply!

Mom's name was mentioned often
  in prayers
  in memories
  in laughter,
  and it helped.

What happened?
  God ordained precious time together,
  Mom close to me,
  Jesus more present,
  gave me what I needed!

I couldn't ignore
  her absence.

I couldn't pretend
  that
  everything was okay!

I couldn't go back
  I had to move
  forward!
  And I did!

OUR ROUND TABLE

January 2, 2014

There's a famous
    old wooden round table
    in the dining room
    at my parent's house.

Mom refinished it to
    a perfect shin,
    bought in Trinidad,
    a beautiful antique.

The never-ending circle
    of that table
    surrounds me with memories
    of Dad's many stories
    Horses
    School pranks
    Cattle

Dancing all over this part of the country
Travel

Of family game time
    Uno
    Gin Rummy
    Mexican Train
    PIP
    Apples to Apples
    Sorry
    Sequence
    Monopoly
    Dad didn't play board games,
    but Mom did,
    and our family did
    and
    does!

Mom and I shared
    heartfelt confessions
    at that table.
    We laughed;
    We cried!

Her favorite meals happened
    when the extension (leaf) was needed
    and the dining room was full.

The meals served there
    fed more than my body
    the laughter
    the conversation
    the teasing.

The food Mom served
    was delicious and tasty.

The deep emotional food
    served at that table
    shaped my life!

Round
    unbroken
    never-ending
    inclusive
    perfect
    That table is home to me!

NINE MONTHS WITHOUT YOU

January 2, 2014

I spent nine months
    growing inside you
    next to your heart
    welcomed

Cherished.
    You knew my every movement!

I now have spent
    nine months without you!

The space in my heart
    cracked
    broken
    empty
    I don't know your movement now!

Your absence resounds in
    my ears and
    echoes through my bones
    and soul!

You bore me
    nurtured me
    grew me to be the
    woman I am today!

In your hour of need,
    I bore you,
    nurtured you yet
    had to let you go!

The paradox of
    mother and daughter
    the flow of life
    the cycle
    fascinates me.

Letting you go
    hurt
    shook my world
    tore me apart!

And here I am,
    nine months without you!
    But you're here
    in my thoughts

in my memories
in my DNA
in your family
in your friends.

You left a strong legacy
  behind!

CAN I GO HOME WITH YOU AND LIN?

January 8, 2014

You were hospitalized
   in Raton
   me in Albuquerque
   working and not able to come sooner.
   The miles between
   stretched too far,
   a long hollow alley
   of separation.

Your few days hospital stay
   filled with several
   phone calls
   to you
   to the various doctors
   to my cousin Janet
   to Jackie,
   our friend
   your caregiver

Finally the weekend arrived.
    Lin and I came
    to help
    as soon as we could!

Your first words to me
    donned in a hospital gown,
    small and frail
    and afraid—

"Can I go home with you and Lin?"

I breathed a
    sigh of relief.

Lin and I had rehearsed
    talked
    and
    rehearsed
    how we were going to
    convince you
    to come home
    with us!

Up until this point
    you were
    an independent
    84-year-old woman
    living alone
    self-sufficient

with help from
    Jackie and Charles.

Our parting after
    Christmas,
    sad.
    You mad at Lin and me.
    I now realize
    you were sick.

Those few days of you
    in the hospital
    in Raton
    miles and hours away
    from me

Those few days for me
    at work
    in Albuquerque
    were torture!

I felt so helpless!
    So lost!

I wanted to help
    and I did, but

I wanted to see your face
    to scan your eyes
    to touch your shoulder
    to hug you.

I wanted to access what was wrong.
    All would be better
    if I could see you.

Thank you
    for needing
    to be with me
    as much as I needed
    to be with you!

Yes, Mom,
    Yes!

We want you with us!
    You are welcome!
    Come home with us.

YOU NEVER KNOW

January 8, 2014

We took you home to Branson, Colorado
    after your hospitalization
    in Raton, New Mexico
    to take you
    to Tijeras, New Mexico
    east of Albuquerque,
    hoping to get better medical care.

You laundered your clothes.
    You rested.
    You visited
    with your precious neighbors.

I called doctors
    in Albuquerque,
    set up appointments,
    trusting to get better care for you.

We took two days
    to do the mundane preparation
    to leave.

Your exit was tearful!
    A sweeping look
    at your home
    for forty-six years,
    your possessions
    the familiar.

I heard your deep knowing sigh
    and words prophetic,
    heart-wrenching!

A stop at the gate,
    With one last glance and sob,
    you said,
    "I wonder if I'll ever be able
    to come back home?"

I assured you!
    Lin joined me with
    comforting words.

You resolutely sat in the back seat,
    buckled in,
    small and overwhelmed with your knowing,
    not looking left or right
    resigned to the fact

that you knew!

Deeply you knew
   and
   somehow
   I did, too!

That you would never be back!
   But who knew?

I WANT YOU BACK! OR DO I?

January 27, 2014

I stand at that mysterious wall
    between life and eternity
    and scream,
    "I want you back!"

I pound my fists.
    I scream!
    I cry,
    but nothing changes.

You slipped
    through my finger tips.

I grasped.

I WANT YOU BACK! OR DO I?

You were here one second
 and
 gone the next!

Nothing I could do
 would hold you.

Where are you now?
 Sitting next to Jesus and Dad—
 smiling
 youthful
 relaxed
 happy!

I hope so!

I am earth bound—
 held in place
 by time and
 my human existence!

I now know more,
 realize there's more.
 There has to be!

A small peephole
 opened into eternity
 at your death bed.

Surprisingly, a small kernel of hope was

born that day for me.

Life ended here for you
 so quickly!

Your shell of a body
 lay limp and lifeless
 in that hospital bed.
 I saw your last breath,
 but I also saw something else
 slight
 faint

Relief for you!
 A passing
 A knowing
 that you are gone
 from here,
 but will wait for me
 there.

In my solemn, desolate space,
 I will still cry,
 "I want you back!"

But today I know
 that
 I don't want you back—

I want to join you
 there!

WHY I READ MY JOURNALS FROM LAST YEAR

February 7, 2014

I journal
    every day I can!

Last year
    during Mom's illness
    Those quiet moments hunched over my journal
    with pen in hand
    centered me
    grounded me
    kept me sane
    saved my life!

This year I reread
    my journals from last year,
    witnessing the struggle
    honoring the woman
    who fought so hard

for Mom and me!

Some people would say
    It's macabre
    insane
    negative
    living in the past

Daily revisiting my words
    my pain
    but I realized today.

I'm honoring the hours
    the minutes
    the seconds
    the time that
    we fought so hard.

I look back now
    with full knowledge.

In the midst of Mom's caregiving,
    I worked,
    Daily
    intense demands from
    my job.

Now I know what the fevers
    in February were—
    leukemia hiding its ugly face
    in obscurity

run rampant!
Bone marrow
Dried and burned out

Now I know what the end
   of life looks like,
   the process of leaving this world
   and going on to the next.

In my journaled words, I see my confusion and sdespair
   in the midst of the
   battle!

I see the valiant effort
   The struggle
   calling me to care for Mom,
   and I did it!

Today fresh tears abound
   as I read my words,
   but I know
   that I won!
   I won me!

I lost my mom,
   but
   I did my best.

And I have witnessed
   this success
   through my journals!

POURED COFFEE ALL OVER MY BOOKS

February 27, 2014

Mom's days in the hospital
    blur now—
    one grueling medical trial
    and tribulation
    after another.

One morning
    like so many others,
    exhausted and driven,
    My brother and I
    do our morning routine.

Up early at 5:20 A.M.—
    write and read
    shower
    breakfast
    drive the eighteen miles to Albuquerque

to the hospital
once more.

In the parking lot
of the hospital
I have a water bottle
in one hand and
a coffee travel mug
in the other—
my roller bag
too.

Instead of putting my
sealed water bottle
in the roller bag,
I put my travel mug
with coffee in it
upside down.

Coffee spews everywhere,
on my journal
on my precious daily meditation books,
everywhere.

So tired
so exhausted
so distracted!

My books' pages
bleed the
coffee stains—
a daily visual reminder

today.

Worn out books,
I have read for years.
dear old friends
pages now stained
with
coffee and
the pain,
the loss of Mom!

FACING ONE YEAR

February 27, 2014

March will be here soon
    and the anniversary
    of the end.

Mom died March 23, 2013
    5:10 P.M.,
    a beautiful spring Saturday evening.

The month of March 2013
    appears as a mere shadow
    to the spring
    that was busting out all over
    New Mexico.

One hospital stay in Raton
    Three hospital stays in Albuquerque

One skilled nursing facility
Bone marrow biopsy

After all this time
FINALLY a diagnosis
A rare form of leukemia
myelofibrosis
A filter to stop the Coumadin
An NG tube because Mom could no longer swallow easily
$10,000 Jakafi—a drug to save her life
Only four pills taken
Hospice that lasted two hours
Death

My brother joined me
to help carry this heavy load!
Daily trips back and forth
to the hospital.
Demanding job in the midst
of this raging insanity.

Visits from loving family and friends
John Dussart
Gerri Dunbar
Cheryl
Rhonda Sandoval
Aunt Willie and Janet
Gary and Diane
Sue, Larraine, Jeff, and Lee-Ann
Cassidy
Jim and Karen
Connie, Emmily, Caden and Kaylea Raye
Lisa
Joan, Diana, Mark, and Zach

My overwhelming tasks
    Orchestrating
    The doctors
    The nurses
    The tests
    The loss of appetite
    The meds
    The visitors
    The hope
    The energy
    My work

I believed
    I worked
    I knew
    Mom would make it,
    but she didn't.

In March,
    the wind blows.
    Prospects of spring foliage
    pop up through
    the dark, dry soil.

It is a season of hope
    birth
    new life

In March,
    we lost Mom!

Dad's birthday
    was March 20.
    Bub and I both feared
    she would die that day!
    That spiritual and emotional tug to him
    and
    heavenward
    would be so strong that day!
    She didn't leave us that day, so we thought
    she would live!

But when March 23 came,
    her soul was heaven bound.
    We saw it when we arrived
    at the hospital
    that fateful morning.

In her eyes,
    riveted to an unknown space heavenward

In her wailing,
    a communication that seared my soul
    In her death!

Dad and Jesus won the battle to take her there—
    Mom's mother, Grandma Dickerson won, too!

ONE YEAR WITHOUT MOM

February 27, 2014

I didn't want to do it!
    I want Mom back.
    I screamed,
    I sobbed uncontrollably
    I cried!

I got sick
    stomach stuff
    I lost 14 pounds
    looked ghastly
    and shriveled

I wanted to die and
    be with Mom.
    I cried.

No more daily phone calls
    to start the morning
    for Mom and me.
    A tradition I started
    after she spent three days alone
    with no electricity
    in a winter storm.
    I cherished that daily communion.

I cried daily now instead!

In June, the annual Branson-Trinchera Reunion came
    Also, my long awaited 60th birthday
    A hollow celebration
    without Mom!
    I cried.

Mom's birthday in September
    We celebrated her
    with Jackie in Branson.
    Mom and Jackie shared the same birth date.
    I cried.

Thanksgiving came.
    We returned to
    the place
    we had celebrated
    with Mom three years ago!
    I cried.

Christmas came!
    Mom was on every gift

I gave.
Pillows
Pillowcases
Every month of our yearly family calendar
Filled with pictures of her!
No new Christmas outfit alike
No ten small Advent gifts
A tradition Mom started twenty-five years ago
to help me through going to treatment
No special gifts from Mom.
I cried.

New Year's Eve came!
    Traditionally, I called Mom every year
    no matter where I celebrated it,
    no matter how late the call.
    I cried.

Mom tucked away in my heart—
    my heart aching for her.

One year is gone.
    My life changed forever.

I cried.

MOM WAS ON EVERY CHRISTMAS GIFT

February 27, 2014

Mom died—
   my first Christmas
   without her
   scared me!

How will I survive?

It ended up being a God Thing
   A miracle
   God's grace!

I survived by putting
   Mom in the midst of
   my gift giving.

I created pillows
 with a special picture
 of Mom
 for that particular person!

I created pillowcases
 with a family picture
 featuring Mom
 for my great-nieces and -nephews,
 even the very young ones
 who knew Mom
 and could hold onto this token of love

Our traditional calendar
 I create every year
 featuring pictures of that year.

This year, it celebrated
 Mom in pictures
 and with
 her words
 her phrases
 her advice
 her humor
 I didn't decide to do this—
 it unfolded!

Many would-be sages' advice about grief:
 Let go
 Don't concentrate on
 your loss
 Pretend
 Don't cry

I couldn't do any of those things!
    Mom was there
    in the gifts
    the memories
    the smiles
    and
    the tears!

I AM ANGRY!

February 27, 2014

It's taken
    almost a year!

I saw an occasional bout
    a wink with the possibility
    a moment
    of anger!

Then waves of grief
    overtook me.

The anger faded
    because the grief took too much energy.
    I couldn't sob and scream obscenities in anger
    at the same time then.

But today
    I am angry!
    And I can do both now.

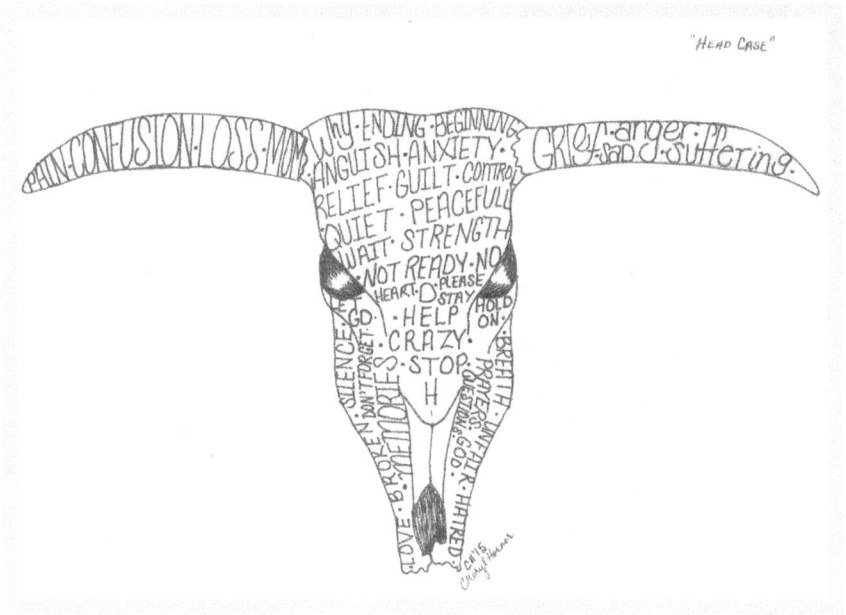

"HEAD CASE"

    Mom didn't have to die,
    to leave us so quickly!
    too early!
    so quickly!

Doctors
    she trusted
    believed in
    betrayed her!

Her hematologist,
    in his complacency,
    let her slip away!

I AM ANGRY!

Ten plus years he treated
    her blood disorder
    warned her
    that it could
    flip flop into
    leukemia.

He didn't demand a bone marrow biopsy,
    a serious, painful test,
    that would have warned us
    of the danger ahead
    and suggested a solution.

After her death,
    I found in her desk drawer
    scribbled on a
    scrap of paper
    "Leukemia."

That possibility haunted her
    always right below the surface of
    her rich, full life
    always ready to rise up
    and scare her at any time!
    The boogieman!

She feared it
    knew it could kill her.

But that doctor ignored

the symptoms
her last year
loss of weight
loss of appetite
altered blood count

Last February,
    when she suffered
    with nightly fevers,
    I called and called him
    repeatedly
    "No connection with her blood disorder,"
    he repeated with authority.

I believed him;
    Bub believed him;
    Mom believed him,
    until his associate
    said differently!

It was too late!
    The leukemia had ravaged
    her body
    like a fire storm
    Her bone marrow
    scarred
    dry
    producing no blood!

Transfusion
    after transfusion!
    Too numerous to count!
    Bruised arms,

I AM ANGRY!

Swollen,
    poked and prodded.

I watched Mom slipping away
    in slow motion!
    I could not stop it!

Frustration
    Despair
    Exhaustion
    Fear
    maximized my
    intensity!

I would save her!
    Screw the doctors!

We got Jakafi,
    An experimental drug
    $10,000 a month
    Outrageous
    but necessary
    the only treatment!

But she was slipping
    Away,
    weaker in this world,
    stronger in the next!

Then she was gone!

Complacency killed her!

A doctor not heeding
    the signs,
    not thinking
    that an 84-year-old woman
    had many more years to live
    not recognizing
    that he
    had threatened
    her for years.

He let ego step in—
    "You took her to Albuquerque.
    She wasn't under my care
    anymore."
    "It wasn't myelofibrosis;
    it was acute leukemia."
    "Blah, blah, blah."
    "It wasn't my fault."

Eleven months later
    I confronted him.

That's what he said—
    "It wasn't my fault.
    I didn't even know she died."

Come on!

Shame on you!

222

I AM ANGRY!

I was calling you
    every week,
    sometimes more often,
    then it ended abruptly!

Come on!

I am angry!
    She was my mother,
    my best friend,
    And you let her die!

Complacency and ego
    blinded you, and
    you sacrificed a precious woman!

I am angry!

I FORGOT MY DAD IN MOM'S OBITUARY

March 20, 2014

Creating Mom's obituary
    Fell on my shoulders,
    my responsibility,
    my task.

I used my sister-in-law Lela's obituary
    as my model,
    in a haze,
    a fog of grief and disbelief,
    and I forgot my dad!

The love of my mom's life
    the heartbeat
    of her soul.

But for seventeen years

after his death,
she lived
she loved
she survived
and
thrived,
and I forgot Dad!

No one else in my family proofread
the obituary.
They trusted me
to do it right.

When I think of it,
I ache to my core!

I feel ashamed;
the guilt covers
my soul
running down into
my shoes,
Paralyzing my every move!

Mom would never
have forgotten Dad!
How could I?

She lived every day
with him on her breath
tucked away in
the corner of her
broken heart,

always there
deeply connected.

But I forgot Dad!

For seventeen years, I
    focused on Mom,
    the individual
    the strong-willed woman
    the ranch manager
    the dancer
    the prankster
    my travel mate
    and
    playmate.

For me, she had outgrown
    the coupleness
    the pairness.

For me, she stood alone,
    a beacon
    a strong woman
    a person
    an individual.

But I forgot Dad!

We added him to
    the obituary read at
    Mom's service.

But the obituary on her program
    doesn't speak of him
    at all
    absent
    silent!

Her forty-three year partner,
    the love of her life!

I'm sorry Mom and Dad;
    I think you understand!

SNUGGLE INTO THE MEMORIES

March 20, 2014

I lost Mom,
    almost one year ago!

Today I sit in her house
    surrounded by her
    and
    snuggle into the memories!

No longer fighting the loss,
    not running away
    from the memories!

Not cringing at
    the empty space
    in my heart.

But I snuggle into the memories,
    lay my head on her shoulder
    like so many times before,
    breathe in her body fragrance
    like so many times before,
    laugh with her—her blue eyes dancing
    like so many times before,
    dance with her around the living room,
    trying to recapture Dad's special step
    like so many times before.

Memories comfort me
    today!
    Hundreds of precious moments
    shared.

I lean into them.

They brush my cheek
    kiss my brow
    caress my shoulder
    live deep in my heart!

I can't bring her back!
    I tried,
    and it doesn't work!
    I can't go with her,
    not yet!

So today
    I snuggle into the memories.
    I speak her name.

I speak her joy.
I speak her laughter.
I speak her fears.
I speak her faith.

I speak Mom!

ONE YEAR

March 23, 2014

It's here!
    One year
    of
    life without Mom!

I can't believe it! I've dreaded it so!
    The anniversary of this life-changing day.

The pain raged;
    the loss roared
    in my heart and soul.

I have never felt
    so alone,
    so orphaned!

During these last three weeks,
 I reread my journals,
 my notes
 from last year
 and marveled—
 How did I do it?

Orchestrating
 doctors
 hospitals
 visitors
 work
 medicine
 Medicare demands
 urgent care visits
 emergency room visits

How did I do it?

Today I mark
 one year—365 days
 I will cry many tears,
 sobs felt all the way
 back to beyond my birth,
 to that time
 when I shared
 Mom's heart
 blood
 body
 spirit

But I will also
 celebrate!

Celebrate
    her life
    our love and
    relationship
    her spirit
    her laughter,
    the nuance of us

She carried me
    nine months
    next to her heart!

I will carry her
    forever
    in my heart!

CAN YOU UNDERSTAND GRIEF?

March 23, 2014

I don't!
   Can you?
   You can't, you say!
   It's not possible!

The best I can do
   Is
   face my life today
   one day at a time!

Shock anesthetized me
   for several weeks!
   I got sick
   undiagnosed stomach pain

that focused me on me
for months.

I attended regular recovery meetings
    grief support groups.

I started a much-awaited retirement.

I devoured books on grief.

I performed the job of "executor of Mom's will"
    and handled the demands of probate.

I managed our family ranch
    four and one half hours away.

I danced.

I fulfilled dance commitments.

A stay-at-home summer
    filled my life,
    but
    the void her absence created
    couldn't be filled.

I questioned

living
I questioned
my God
I questioned
everything!

My core was rattled
    so many
    unanswered questions
    I had never thought of before.

The best I could do
    was
    cry!

Special days
    and
    anniversaries
    came and went
    with apprehension
    and I cried more!

Memorial Day with a visit
    to Mom's grave, flowers and tears

My 60th birthday—a day Mom so
    wanted to celebrate
    and

The Fourth of July—a tradition broken

this first year
because Bub and I couldn't endure it
without
Mom
Mom's birthday—celebrated with Jackie
in Branson—so sad and hollow

Then the holidays

Halloween—she loved the kids dressed up and
    prepared treats each year.
    Trinidad people sat in her drive way and handed out candy—
certainly a God Thing!

Thanksgiving—return to the place we had been a couple years ago,
this time
    without Mom
    Christmas—in her home
    and she in the midst of the gifts
    New Year's Eve—numb and hollow

Then 2014
    facing the first anniversary of
    Mom's death

The best I could do
    was
    cry and write!

Grief is a process!
    messy

cyclical
scary
overwhelming,
and it's mine!

And I don't understand it!

WHERE IS SHE? HOW IS SHE?

March 23, 2014

Where is Mom?
    Pressing in
    from her side of eternity
    face near the invisible divider
    between this life and the next
    trying to comfort me
    with her sweet, soft words
    trying to hold me
    with her out-stretched hand!

Fingertips trace my full name
    on that divider,
    words I can't see from this side.

Is she sitting on a cloud resting
    after a jitterbug with Dad to "In the Mood,"
    catching her breath?

Does she have two beautiful, slim legs
    and feet—
    the swelling gone
    her mangled left foot
    perfect and wearing
    pretty 3 1/2-inch-spiked heels
    like she loved in her
    younger days?

Is there blood flowing freely
    throughout her body?
    enough red and white blood cells—
    no more transfusions?

Are her arms smooth and pink,
    free from needles, injections,
    and bruises?

Has she thrown away her eyeglasses
    and her eyedrops for glaucoma
    to see clearly the beauty around her?

Has she crocheted hundreds of
    beautiful afghans
    out of wispy clouds and colorful dreams
    with straight pain-free fingers?

Has she danced in Dad's arms
    nonstop for a year and
    her feet never hurt?

Her heart rejoicing
looking up into his eyes
so happy to be together
once again
on the dance floor!

Does she sing her favorite hymns
    at the alter of her God,
    voice loud and clear
    with her mother and dad
    and her family and friends?

Did her family
    and dear friends
    who went before her circle close around her
    and celebrate her passage into their arms?

Did Dad and Mom square dance a tip
    to Marvin Schilling
    the minute she arrived?

The after life
    the other life
    remains a mystery!

But I believe this all
    is possible!

I can hardly wait to see
    Mom
    like this!

THAT DAY—I CAN HARDLY WAIT!

March 23, 2013

From March 23, 2013
    I have looked forward
    to that day—
    The day I see Mom
    again!

Possibly years to go—
    I don't know!
    I will anticipate it,
    yearn for it
    prepare for it.

When it happens,
    I will celebrate!

I will move seamlessly

from here to there!
I will not fight it,
nor hold onto this mortal life.

The moment it happens,
I will go to sleep here,
and
I will wake up there!

I will jump up
from my bed
race to my Jesus
arms extended
and scream for joy!

I will hear my name
floating on the air.
It will be Him shouting
my name!

I will recognize His voice.
His arms will wrap around me
so familiar
so full of love!

And standing beside Him
tugging at his sleeve
whispering my name
tapping me on the shoulder
will be Mom and Dad.

The hug I get then
    from them
    will erase all the tears
    I shed,
    all the pain and sorrow

And behind them,
    family and friends will circle
    me with love
    greeting me
    with hugs, kisses, sighs, and laughter!

And I will be truly home at last—

I can hardly wait!

WHY DELAY MOM'S FUNERAL?

April 2, 2014

Mom died on March 23, 2013.
    Her service was delayed
    until April 1—nine days!

"Not the best way to handle grief!"
    my sister Sue warned.

Originally we wanted the service
    on March 30
    A Saturday
    but Trinidad Masonic Cemetery,
    a small town,
    doesn't bury on Saturdays
    wouldn't open a grave on Saturday!

Shocked, we moved it to Friday

March 29.
That would work.

But something nagged at my spirit,
    Memory below consciousness.
What was it?

Our lives had run at a hectic pace
    for weeks.

I checked email regularly,
    trying to keep connected to my world,
    trying to keep family and friends
    informed about Mom's progress
    but didn't remember specifics
    right now.

I ran upstairs to my computer.

I checked my emails
    Alice Unwin,
    a dear friend from Kim, Colorado
    who shared Mom's birthday
    who shared the same class ring design
    who was a longtime friend
    was scheduled to be buried on
    Friday, March 30
    at 10:00 A.M.
    in Kim, Colorado
    fifty miles away.

Could we have Mom's at 1:00 P.M.
    or
    2:00 P.M.
    in Trinidad,
    Fifty plus miles away
    the same day?

What do I do?
    A dilemma?

Again my spirit said,
    "No!"

But I needed confirmation,
    assurance,
    so I called our family friend Lolly Ming
    for her opinion
    and she agreed.

"It will force people to choose!
    Don't ask friends
    to choose;
    besides they were dear friends.
    No, no—not a good idea!"

So Monday, April 1, 2013
    we buried Mom
    enough time for the California family
    to get here
    enough time to celebrate
    Easter with our family
    enough time to cry

to mourn
to write her eulogy
to spend time in Branson
to visit with friends.

So was it coincidentally on April 1?
    Helen Waldroup's birthday,
    her best friend for many years
    April Fools' Day
    for a woman who
    love a good practical joke!
    God's sense of humor!

Why the delay?
    Because God planned it
    that way!

And I listened!

MOM'S SERVICE

April 2, 2014

The plan came together.
    I knew to look
    Andy and I searched and searched for
    a written outline
    a clue
    What do you want, Mom?

Nestled in her well-worn Bible,
    Specific Scriptures identified to be read
    at her funeral
    Psalms 150
    Ecclesiastes 3:1-8
    2 Timothy 3:16-17
    Strong statements of
    her deep Christian beliefs
    and her love of dance.

Bub, Andy, and I sat
    at our round table
    in Branson, Colorado
    Brainstorming
    what else.

What music?

It hit me like a thunderbolt.
    I heard Mom's voice so often:
    "I want 'Stardust' played at my funeral."
    "Stardust"
    Mom's repeated words echoed in my memory!

I pushed to have a lively polka played
    when our family entered the chapel,
    and Bub reluctantly agreed.
    A weekly Saturday ritual of Mom's
    Molly B's Polka Party
    She danced around the living room
    by herself
    remembering the long-gone days in Dad's arms.

I called Sam Bachicha,
    musician and family friend,
    to sing.
    The only one who could!
    The only one we wanted.
    He sang at Dad's service.

So it was.
    Big Band music played

256

before the service.
Music that Mom and Dad had loved
and danced too often.

One picture of Mom on the screens
    on each side of the chapel.
    Another one of her wishes honored—
    no PowerPoint slideshow of pictures.
    No easel display full of pictures o her.

Our family walked into the chapel
    To
    "The Beer Barrel Polka!"
    Chuckles from family and
    friends who knew Mom's weekly ritual!

Adrianne, Mom's minister, led the touching service.
    My husband, Lin, read Mom's story:
    Her Eulogy
    Mom's history with lots of funny poignant stories
    Group participation questions
    My poem about Mom

The drive to the cemetery in the limousine
    with family and a friend is a blur.

At the cemetery,
    Sobs gathered in my throat
    when I saw the open grave—
    the end,
    the finality.
    How could we put her in the ground?

It felt so harsh and callous.
I wanted her with me.

My eyes were riveted on that empty grave.
    My sister tried to distract me,
    but she couldn't.

It ended here.

A simple service
    Graveside
    Ashes to ashes,
    Dust to dust!

A reverent grave worker
    knelt in prayer and waited for us to leave.

Friends hugged me,
    consoled me,
    wrapped me up in their love,
    their comfort.

A dinner at the Community Center
    in Branson, Colorado.
    provided by the community,
    tradition that my mom had
    participated in often.
    Food and fellowship
    and a hole in my heart!

SORTING MOM'S CLOTHES AND STUFF

October 7, 2014

A mound of your clothes
    sit in the middle
    of your bed!

My bed now!

Clothes I've decided
    to give away
    to Goodwill.

A colorful array tossed together
    sweaters mostly
    some t-shirts
    some jeans

Your precious clothes
    thrown in a heap!

I knew you in each outfit,
    each colorful blouse,
    each t-shirt and
    and memories overflowed.

How do I start this?
    How do I go through your things?
    Private items.

It's been nineteen months,
    and I still feel
    paralyzed
    when I think about it.

Last year before Christmas
    I gave your Christmas outfits
    like mine
    away
    to a friend
    who had lost everything
    she owned in a fire!

My heart wrenched as I gathered
    them, but I did it anyway.

At the same time,
    I collected your coats
    for a coat drive

at church
before the cold of
winter set in.
Your coats warmed homeless women.

But now,
    It's everything else!
    Jeans
    Slacks
    Blouses
    Dresses!
    Memorabilia!
    There's so much!

My solution
    to this gigantic task?

One room at a time,
    One drawer at a time!

I can't do it all at once.
    No way!

As long as your dresses hang
    in the closet,
    your blouses, too!
    your perfume on each piece of clothing,

You are still here,
    and it helps me!

THE POEMS DWINDLED!

January 16, 2015

My second holiday season without Mom—
    Halloween
    Thanksgiving
    Christmas
    have passed!

I cried.

I celebrated!

I spent less time
    looking back and aching,

more time looking forward

This Christmas,
    I created a family gift about Mom
    A cookbook
    Volume 1
    Pies, Cakes and Candy
    Fun-loving pictures of her
    on the cover and
    inside.

It featured her famous pie crust recipe,
    given to Mom by Dr. Barglow's wife,
    Dated 1952.

I got to see her smile,
    Touch the recipe cards
    she handled hundreds of times,
    enjoyed her handwriting
    and whimsical notes.

It healed me deeply.

It's not over!

The pain and loss continues,
    but

today

she is present in my heart

and life
in a different way.

And that is enough
for now,
until I see her again!

VISITING HOME AGAIN

January 21, 2015

After an emotional afternoon
 of clearing out more of
 Mom's clothes,
 I relaxed on the couch
 and
 napped,
 maybe the first time
 since Mom passed.

My favorite napping spot—
 a light blanket
 covered me.

When I woke, I opened my eyes, missing it!
 Mom's kitchen sounds
 preparing dinner
 cooking.

So often in the past,
    Mom in her favorite spot
    cooking in the kitchen

The sounds echoed
    through my memory
    spoons clatter against a pot
    the fridge door opens and closes
    the mixer sings as it works
    and so does Mom
    plates rattle as she gets them out of the cabinet
    silverware clank as she gathers them from the drawer.

Then Mom's often-repeated comment to wake me,
    "Larada, wake up.
    Dinner's ready."

Luscious sounds—
    I heard those sounds

often
    asleep or awake

As I napped
    on that couch
    deep in my subconscious
    my heart heard
    Mom's kitchen sounds
    safe
    protective

care-taking

Our family setting

Before Dad died,
    he sat near
    in his favorite recliner
    reading or
    watching TV.
    Comforted in his nearness
    and silence.

But not there now.

When I woke,
    I knew something was missing!

The kitchen was silent,
    Dad's chair sat empty,

and I missed Mom and Dad!

EVERYONE NEEDS AN ADVOCATE

February 6, 2015

I tried and tried
    to keep you alive.

Here it is, February again!
    Two years ago this month
    you battled nightly fevers.
    Never having children,
    I didn't know what to do.

Your general practitioner
    had no answer,
    so I Googled it.
    What do I do?

Your hematologist
    had no answer.

What a red flag it was
knowing what I know now.

I tried and tried
    to keep you alive!

I researched on the Internet
    what to do for fevers:
    Ice chips to munch on,
    Cold washcloths on your forehead
    Two Tylenol pills every four hours

What to do?
    What to do?

During the month of February,
    fevers
    consumed us—
    and more fevers!
    Raging fevers in the night
    Calm down during the day

I continued my research on the Internet;
    could it be leukemia?
    I saw it referenced often.
    What Mom feared
    the most!

I tried and tried to
    keep you alive,
    but you were too sick,

too gone.

"Your bone marrow
    looked like it had
    been ravished by a fire,
    producing no blood!"

It was leukemia!

I fought
    Bub fought

Death and leukemia won,
    But
    Mom knew
    we fought!

I AM PARALYZED TWO YEARS LATER

February 2015

I am paralyzed!
　　Lethargic.

I went to a funeral
　　of a dear family friend
　　in Raton, New Mexico
　　and
　　cried the fifty-mile drive
　　home
　　to Branson, Colorado.

It will be two years in March
　　since Mom died.

A speck of time
　　compared to eternity,

Two short, lonely, long drawn out years.

But it seems like
    forever
    since
    I touched Mom,
    smelled her familiar fragrance,
    heard her laughter.

A lifetime
    since she was carefree,
    giggling.

Mom's infectious laughter
    lit up a room!

I have grieved
    I have mourned,
    and I thought I was done!

No way!

WHAT DOES TWO YEARS LOOK LIKE?

March 22, 2015

It's March.
    An uneasiness drapes my shoulders
    like a familiar acquaintance.

I know it's coming.
    I know the power of painful anniversaries,
    sad memories,
    but here I am caught,
    unprepared!

It's the second anniversary
    of Mom's death.
    Yesterday
    Saturday,
    the day of the week

she passed
always an important day in
The Horner family
so I danced.

Tomorrow is the actual date of her death
 March 23—

I've worked.
 I've healed.
 I've focused on living,
 yet honoring Mom.

I've visited her grave
 often
 and felt relief and pain
 at her graveside.

I've cried
 sobbed
 written
 wailed,

and here it is again!

A wave of pain and loss
 wash over me,
 taking my breath away!

I tell my husband my pain.

I call my brother
to share the pain.
I need to talk to people
who knew her,
who loved her.

Oh, how I miss her!

FEBRUARY FEVERS

December 18, 2015

February 2013
    Fevers
    nightly!
    Skip one night or two
    Yeah, we're done!

Back with a vengeance
    103
    104
    101

Daytime—
    exhausted from the night
    before
    and no fever.

As the day progressed
    and darkness fell once more,
    anxiety mounted about the coming night

Queries and questions
    of the doctors.
    What is it?
    Why?
    What causes it?

Never having had children,
    I went to the Internet!

"What do you do for a fever?"
    Cool washcloths
    Suck on ice chips
    Tylenol
    So we did these,
    but the fevers continued!

Weeks went by!
    Repeated phone calls
    to doctors

Does this have to do
    with Mom's blood disorder,
    polycythemia vera?
    No, from her general practitioner.
    No, from her hematologist.
    No! said the doctors.

The basic feeling I sensed
    from them
    after so many repeated calls:
    Don't bother me.
    Not that important.
    Stop calling.

Back to the Internet
    with more research
    and a word repeated in each search results:
    leukemia

Oh, no
    Mom's biggest fear.

Lin scoured the Internet,
    and he found the same
    word repeated.
    I never told her what I found!

Then one lucky night,
    another evening phone call,

The partner of Mom's hematologist answered the phone.
    His inspired question,
    "When did she have her last bone marrow biopsy?"
    "She's never had one!"

I heard a resounding gasp
    on the other end of the line.

I tucked this piece of information
    away
    for later.

The fevers continued.

It was a cold February
    with a strategic plan in place:
    how to get Mom to
    the emergency room
    with the least
    amount of waiting time!

Saturday morning,
    end of February,
    after yet another bout with the nightly fever,
    prepared and ready to go
    at 8:00 A.M.

It worked,
    and they admitted her.

Finally, I had help.

Finally, someone listened.

Finally, an answer,
    but not one I was
    prepared for
    at all!

WE RELEASED MOM

December 18, 2015

That Saturday morning,
    Mom's eyes stared at
    the ceiling
    and beyond.

Vacant, otherworldly.

No words,
    only groans
    moans
    wails.

Discouraging words from her doctor—
    possible brain damage,
    possibly the end!

With Bub on one side
    of Mom's bed
    and me on the other,

We whispered release as
    tears fell!

"Mom, it's okay to go!
    We'll be okay.
    We'll miss you,
    but it's time.
    Dad's calling your name.
    Jesus stands
    ready
    with arms outstretched!

Go to them!
    It's okay!
    Yes, we'll miss you.
    Desperately,
    but it's okay.
    Go!"

In less than six hours,
    she breathed her last!
    The prayer of release,
    Catherine Marshall taught me
    years ago,
    worked again.

A selfish spirit
    can keep a person

here, on this side,
bound by his or her desires
or needs
when someone may be ready
to go!

For an instant, I stopped.
    I knew the power of this prayer.

I didn't want to lose her—
    NO!!!
    But,
    I knew she was ready.

I wasn't.
    Bub wasn't,
    but she was,
    So we let her go!

And God did the rest!

MOM HID A PAIR OF MY PANTIES

January 28, 2016

When I went home to visit,
    Mom loved to spoil me
    do my laundry
    fix my favorite meal
    let me nap on the couch
    while she prepared her special meal.

What a wonderful experience!

The week after she died,
    I needed to touch her clothes.

I went through every drawer
    her t-shirts
    her underwear
    her jeans

her bras.

I could smell her fragrance,
    that smell that was Mom.

In one drawer,
    I found a pair of my white panties
    folded neatly
    tucked away
    in the back.

I gasped
    I sobbed

I screamed for my brother.

"These are my panties.
    She kept a pair of my panties."

I was shocked,
    but as the surprise wore off,

I smiled,
    I giggled.

I knew that she had wanted to keep
    a part of me with her.

After Dad died, any time I left,
    she cried.

She tried so hard not to—
    Me, too!
    We would hug,
    and then we would sob,
    clinging to each other
    to postpone my departure.

So a pair of my panties became
    an easy way to keep me there.

Her love ran so deep!
    And those panties confirmed that for me!

ONE FOOT HERE AND ONE FOOT THERE

January 28, 2016

In my sixty plus years,
    I have lost so many dear people
    Family and friends
    They have gone *there*, ahead of me.

My first loss was Granddad Horner
    when I was in the sixth grade.

Then I lost my other three grandparents.
    I watched my parents grieve
    the loss of their parents,
    fearing the day that I would lose mine,
    yet young enough to think it was a long time off.

As a young adult, my aunt Helen died at fifty-six years old,
    way too young.

I watched how my cousins mourned the loss of
their mother,
how they cared for her,
and I took note.

For many years, I feared Dad's death,
    his presence so large in my life,
    but I survived
    by focusing on Mom
    and her needs,
    by focusing on my recovery
    and staying close to my program.

But his death reminded me
    that there was another place—*there*
    that I didn't understand
    but knew was different
    from *here*.

As the years have passed more have gone *there*.
    Roy McMillan
    Uncle Hughie
    Uncle Tanky
    Mokey McMillan
    Fred Horner
    Lela
    Linda Prichard
    Kathi Raver
    Reu
    Helen
    Then my best friend, Candy, died.

I began to feel that

I had more loved ones
over *there*
than *here*.

Mom's death plunged me deeply
into this awareness.

I wondered how she was *there*,
what was it like *there*?

All of a sudden,
I felt that I had more interest *there*
than *here*.

I told my therapist this idea.
She said
"Isn't that what we are here for?"

So
I look forward to going *there*.
I won't miss *here*.

A loving familiar crowd will greet me,
I am sure!

I FELT LIKE AN ADULT ORPHAN

February 5, 2016

Dad died in 1996.
 My life had always
 been deeply connected to his.

I bounced many important ideas
 off of him.
 We danced.
 We traveled.
 We enjoyed the ranch together.
 I visited often.
 Dad and Mom visited
 my home often.
 We spent many holidays together.
 We enjoyed each other.

After his death,
    alone
    lonely,
    but I had Mom!

For seventeen years
    I had Mom.
    We shared
    more deeply.
    We grieved the loss of Dad
    together.
    We traveled,
    a once-in-a-lifetime trip
    to Eastern Europe
    in 1999.
    We played!

After a horrible snowstorm
    in 2006,
    she had been snowed in
    all alone
    for three days
    with no electricity.
    She sat in the dark illumined by kerosene lamps.
    She talked to no one.
    She saw no one
    for those three days.

I made a vow after that horrible experience!
    I WOULD CALL HER EVERY MORNING!

I worked hard at keeping that
    commitment!

So our ritual
became a precious time
for her
and
me!

After she died,
   A friend said, "Is your dad dead?'
   I responded, "Yes!"
   "Do you feel like an orphan?"
   I gasped!
   Something shifted in me,
   "Yes, I do!"

ORPHAN
   "a child who has lost both parents through death, or, less
commonly, one parent."

Yes, I was an orphan—an adult orphan.
   Unsheltered
   Vulnerable
   Unprotected

For the first time in my life,
   The adult,
   The oldest generation!

What a shock!

"AMAZING GRACE" PLAYED ON MY IPAD

August 25, 2016

Can a song keep Mom here?
    How do I comfort her?
    How do I hold onto her?

I found "Amazing Grace" on Pandora
    and placed my iPad
    on her pillow
    near her right ear.

The moans continued.
    She showed no sign of recognition.

"Mom, this is your favorite hymn!"

Nothing!

The end was coming.
    I could feel it,
    smell it,
    taste its bitterness in my mouth.

How do I keep her here?
    How do I comfort her?

Maybe Mom's favorite song, "Amazing Grace,"
    would do the trick.

Often I had heard her sing that song
    in church.

Her throaty voice was delightful to me
    but to others
    maybe a scratchy noise.

Would that song hold her here
    or
    release her to her ultimate destination?

Mom showed no sign, but I knew—
    It comforted her.
    It comforted me.

The familiar hymn echoed
    through that small hospice room

and I knew that
her parents,
Granddad and Grandma Dickerson,
sang it on the other side
to draw her home.

The song played.
   I didn't keep her here,
   but
   I played her favorite Christian hymn,
   and it comforted her.

The melody still fills
   my heart with Mom.

TIME TO CRY EACH DAY

August 25, 2016

Is there an appropriate time to cry?
    An appropriate way to mourn?

I didn't know how.

At first, the tears would come unannounced
    in a flurry,
    and I was gone.
    Sobs!

I never knew when or where.
    They consumed my day,
    flooding me with emotion.

I dreaded the next outburst.

I couldn't control the tears.

A grief counselor's suggestion:
    "Appoint a time every morning
    to cry,"
    so I did.

I did my morning writing and reading
    with my cat, Jesse.
    Then I cried
    and cried
    and cried.

Does that sound fake?
    manufactured?
    manipulated?

I don't know,
    but it worked for me!

At first the tears came whenever,
    a trigger
    a memory,
    and I cried.

After awhile,
    knowing I had that special time
    alone with Jesse
    every morning
    relieved me the rest of the day.

I might get choked up,
     but I would say to myself,
     "Save it for the morning."
     I did,
     And it worked!

DENIAL AND MOM'S FUNERAL

August 25, 2016

I never mentioned the "F" word
    to Mom.

I never thought it
    while she was alive.

My focus was
    all-consuming
    total—
    I was going to keep her alive.

Death wasn't a possibility

Now I see the denial.
    Was it wrong?

Was it stupid?
I don't think so.

In tough times,
    I operate on
    a deep knowing
    a spiritual connection.

Denial helped me
    keep going
    keep doing the work I need to do
    to keep Mom alive.

I had one mission,
    one task,
    and I put all my energy
    into it.

The sad part is
    I didn't talk to Mom
    about her funeral.

Oh, yes, we had talked about it for years.
    She wanted "Stardust" played.
    She didn't want all the pictures and hoopla,
    but that was it.

At the end of her life,
    it never crossed my mind.
    It wasn't a possibility, yet,
    and I am okay with that.

LIVE ONE WORLD AT A TIME

August 25, 2016

In recovery,
    we say, "One Day at a Time."

In my life after Mom's death,
    I say, "One World at a Time."

My feet walk this earth,
    planted firmly on sandstone and among chollas
    in the scenic Southwest.

My heart yearns for another world,
    that heavenly place
    that houses so many dear ones.

I am *here*;

they are *there*.

Sometimes I feel their pull
    to that other place,
    a spiritual calling
    attached to my heart.

I resist.

I focus on today
    this world.

My full, rich life *here*,
    and the resistance quiets.

My job today
    and as long as I am *here*,
    is one world at a time!

SUBWAY SANDWICHES REMIND ME OF MOM

August 25, 2016

Triggers,
    reminders of Mom caught me off guard
    for quite awhile.

Smells took my breath away.

Passing the hospital where Mom died,
    choked me up for years.

Hearing "Stardust"
    or
    "Amazing Grace"
    caused the tears and renewed my grief.

A couple weeks ago,

Lin and I stopped at a Subway
　　to eat.

I was catapulted back
　　to that Subway
　　in the hospital
　　where Mom died.

Many sad and tired meals shared
　　across from my brother
　　or
　　Alone.

The smell of turkey
　　and roast beef
　　Standing in line and
　　reading the menu
　　again
　　and again,
　　trying to decide
　　which sandwich
　　to buy
　　seemed monumental
　　in light of the pain carried.

Grief comes and goes.
　　It comes back when you least
　　expect it.

What causes the regression back?
　　A smell
　　A song

A touch

I don't know what brings it up again,
　　Suddenly
　　With no warning
　　years later.

But I do know that
　　it is real!

MY DOCTOR DIDN'T TOUCH ME

August 25, 2016

Lin and I took Mom to her home from the hospital
    in Raton.

A dear neighbor came to visit,
    to console Mom
    in her sickness.

They started to discuss
    their doctor because
    they had the same doctor.

The comment they both shared
    broke my heart,
    "He never touches me."

Two elderly women identified
    A need
    A desire
    we all have—
    To be touched,
    especially when we are sick.

I couldn't believe it.
    They elaborated
    and shared more.

I took it all in
    and decided on a doctor test.

I shared it with Mom,
    and she agreed.

We were headed to Albuquerque
    near to where I live.
    She needed a new general physician,
    a doctor that would touch her.

So off to the doctor we went.
    She sat up on the examination table
    and cried.

He cuddled her in his arms
    and said, "We need to find out
    what's wrong with you!"

Through her tears, Mom looked at me over his shoulder
    and winked.

He had passed the test—
    He touched her.

And he did it every visit
    after that!

AN ANGEL FROG

November 14, 2016

My mom loved frogs.
    Doris Goff started her collection.

She had many—
    dancing frog statues
    a lady frog with
    voluptuous lips
    and long eyelashes
    a furry musical group of frog singers
    a mobile of green creatures.

I asked my niece to illustrate
    this book.
    She added an angel frog
    to her drawings.

My heart leapt.

My mom sent this green angel as a sign
    to care
    and
    protect
    her loved ones.

His tears fall for
    our pain in
    the loss of Mom,
    daily life losses.

Mom, you are still here
    in your angel frog!

TIME AT MOM'S AND DAD'S GRAVES

January 19, 2017

A winter snowy blanket covers
    the ground around
    your gravestones!

A quiet, restful peace
    dry and crisp grass
    needed moisture.

The weathered artificial flowers remain
    from Memorial Day last—

my focus has changed.

I prided myself
    in changing the flowers

every couple months
the first couple years.

Not this last year!

No Christmas poinsettias,
    No holly or a wreath
    from Christmas 2016.

But here I am
    2017
    sitting in my car
    near your graves,
    near you once again!

More tears than I've shed
    in months.

Again,
    a torn apart heart!

This solitary place
    soothes my soul.

Day to day
    I rush
    I hurry
    I do
    I overdo!

Here I just am.
    I'm quiet.
    I listen to your silent message.
    I cry.
    I pray.

I'm your daughter,
    missing you two.

Precious memories tumble
    over each other
    Laughter
    Dances
    Hugs
    Your far-reaching love.

Here I just am!
    No hurry
    Just us
    communing again
    in the quiet!

This tradition
    embedded
    in my spirit.

You visited the dead.
    You visited cemeteries,
    not morbid reflection.

You taught me

take the time,
honor all of your relations
and just be
and

I need this!

HONORING THE DEAD

February 27, 2017

As a child,
    Memorial Day was a ritual,
    a day to honor the dead.

So we visited the cemetery in
    Des Moines, New Mexico.

Often we met Mom's parents
    from Amarillo, Texas
    and Aunt Willie and Uncle Hughie
    from Albuquerque, New Mexico.

The community gathered,
    cleaned up around their family graves—
    rakes, hoes, and trash bags.

As children,
>   we raced around,
>   playing with local kids,
>   meeting new friends.

Adults gathered,
>   talked,
>   visited,
>   after the family grave was cleaned.

A time to honor those gone,
>   a time to stop,
>   a tradition.

Often we headed to Amarillo
>   to spend a week with our grandparents
>   and Mom,
>   a time to celebrate the living.

But first we stopped
>   and honored our dead!

MOM'S STUFF AND HOUSE TODAY

April 9, 2017

I got rid of most of Mom's clothes,
    donations to Goodwill,
    select items to friends.

But I kept a few memorable items—
    A couple t-shirts
    A warm up set
    Her nightgowns
    Her robes
    To wear them is to feel her arms around me.

I've kept her house the same
    for the most part
    knick knacks fill her China closet
    Frog statues grace spots in each room

familiar homemade dish rags to wash our dishes,
a sweet throw draped on the sofa
from her sister
lauding sisterhood.

I did add a new bedspread
    to her bed,
    my bed now.
    A quilt made of her
    favorite t-shirts and blouses
    edged in purple,
    a nice addition.

I brought my wicker hanging basket chair,
    a feature of my home since the 70s
    a piece of me added to my house now.

I remembered Mom had some renovations she wanted
    but didn't get to do, so I did:
    New kitchen floor
    New windows
    Door to the basement
    Painted the exterior

I looked around and saw other renovations I wanted,
    so I did:
    Added a patio area out back
    New front porch

I love the mixture of
    Dad's, Mom's, and mine.
    It makes the house mine now!

OUR WEEKLY APPOINTMENT

May 26, 2017

I don't know when it started,
    but I looked forward to it
    each Sunday night.
    A weekly telephone call to Mom
    on my way home
    from my AA meeting.

Yes, we talked every morning
    on my way to work
    during the week
    since 2006,
    but this weekly appointment—
    somehow was different.

In 2005, my brother's wife passed away,
    and I added him to my Sunday routine.
    I called him on the way to the meeting

and caught up with him.

I called Mom on the way home
    to end the trip—
    nice bookends to
    my trip.

Precious moments of laughter and life shared.

When Mom died,
    I asked Aunt Willie if I could call her
    on Sunday evenings.
    "Of course!" She said!

So the last four years, I have called,
    and hearing her voice
    reminds me of Mom.

Precious moments of laughter and life shared.

Chapter Eleven

THE FIRST YEAR FOLLOWING MOM'S DEATH: APRIL 2013 – MARCH 2014

Those first weeks after Mom's death blurred into one big heartache. For this book, I have used a mixture of my sketchy memory and factual information taken from my daily journals to chronicle the years afterwards. Since the early nineties, I have written "Morning Pages," a suggestion from Julia Cameron's *The Artist's Way* of writing three pages long-hand each morning of whatever is going on in your life at the time. They've come in handy on a number of occasions as a reference point.

I re-entered my normal life and went back to work. After focusing on Mom for three months, I felt lost, but I knew that I had to listen to my spirit on how to grieve. Plus I kept hearing in my mind Mom's advice about what to do.

I went to bed each night with the hustle and bustle of the day behind me. In the dark and quiet, I snuggled close to Lin and cried. My grief flooded me in the dark and I sobbed, I talked, and he listened—exactly what my aching heart needed. This became a nightly routine.

Probably because of my involvement in twelve-step programs for many years, immediately, I searched out grief support groups in Albuquerque. I attended one at the Jewish center and found comfort in being in a room full of people who were grieving a loss of some kind. The one drawback was there were people there who had attended that group for years. I didn't see myself attending a grief support group forever, so the basis of that group concerned me, but it helped me get started.

I only went there for a couple weeks, until the hospice where Mom had died contacted me about a grief support group starting. I decided to switch groups, and it saved my life. It was smaller than the Jewish group, and I thrived there. Again it was a room of broken hearts mourning a loss, but everyone's loss was fresh and recent.

The counselor at this group gave out helpful handouts at every meeting, and I used all of them. Then she gave us the opportunity to share what was going on for us—powerful personal sharing and tears. The tears shed by others validated my tears that flowed freely there. I could relate to each and every one in the group. I attended regularly for about six to nine months then felt like I was ready to move on—I truly believe it saved my life.

My normal routine helped me so much to deal with my loss of Mom. I am secretary for the Branson-Trinchera reunion, an annual reunion for our small country school, and I have been on that committee since 1993. Because of Mom's sickness and the death of Jack Gilstrap, the committee president's father, we toyed with the idea of minimizing the activities for the event that year. We were behind in planning, and the suggestion was given to help lessen our stress.

I went to bed crying after that discussion, wanting to keep this special event the same in a year that had been so unusual and painful for me. The committee ended up doing exactly what we had done for many years.

I filled the immediate weeks after Mom passed with preparation for an annual square and round dance event, Duke City Singles and Doubles Square Dance Festival. I was chairperson of the festival, and it gave me something outside my pain to focus on during this hard, hard time. It felt good to complete that commitment I had made, and Mom so enjoyed all my involvement in the square dance world.

At the event, I gave each of the committee members and the calling and cuing staff a memento connected to my mom—a solar-activated plastic flower with bees and ladybugs on it—very cheesy.

My cousin Janet had given Mom one the previous spring, and Mom proudly displayed it in her kitchen window over the sink. I spied them at a store before the festival and bought them. In my grief, I had to have my mom present there to ease my pain.

The next weekend on Mother's Day, at the end of our state square and round dance festival, I curled up on the bed at our motel with severe stomach cramps, after having diarrhea. My stomach problems began. I lost fourteen pounds quickly because I couldn't eat without severe pain and missed a lot of work.

I wondered if I was dying. At times, I hoped I was. All seemed useless. I spent countless hours in bed with my stomach pain and a heating pad, trying to ease the pain. I started a series of tests to try to figure it out.

At first, I couldn't write—I was numb and barely existing. My stomach pain scared me. But in early May my poetry writing started! Each poem seemed to release a small part of the solid block of pain in my soul.

Monthly I shared the grief poems I had written with my therapist. She knew I was a writer and encouraged me to continue writing poetry because she saw the healing power in writing for me, plus she valued the poetry that expressed my emotions. Early on, she suggested I publish a book of my grief poetry.

One particular night after reading a series of poems I had written that month, she wiped a tearful eye and challenged me, "Promise you will publish these poems so my daughters can read them when I am gone and receive the help that you got in writing them."

For the first few months, every fourth Saturday at 5:10 P.M., I would look at the clock, put on makeup to go out dancing, and cry. Saturday had always been a dance night in the Horner family, so Mom's death on an early Saturday evening was so appropriate because she joined Dad again, but so painful as I relived it.

After one of my recovery meetings where I had shared my struggles with my grief once again, a dear friend suggested I add something to my quiet time each morning. She suggested, "Invite your Mom to join you for the day." It sounds so simple but it has been so refreshing to do that.

Returning to the cemetery in Trinidad, I decorated Mom's and Dad's graves for Memorial Day—a tradition that had been engrained in me my whole life. I also put out flowers on my grandparents' graves and Dad's sister's grave.

My health issues monopolized most of May and June.

For years, I had wondered about the value of yoga. An online discount offering sent me a discount on a yoga class, so I attended one. I was searching for anything that would help me deal with the over-whelming physical and emotional pain.

The instructor queried me about my reason for coming. I told her that I had just lost my mother. She told me she was writing a book about Yoga and Grief and that people suffering grief had to deal with "the will to live" after a loss.

Many of the days I had spent in bed with severe cramps and sick, I felt like I had the option to die. Often I thought it would be easier to die. She struck a nerve with me.

Years before, I had been diagnosed with GERD (gastroesophageal reflux disorder), but I didn't have any of the usual symptoms and I took no medication, so I had dismissed it as a misdiagnosis.

Finally I received a diagnosis for my stomach pain. After testing, I was diagnosed with GERD again and something else: celiac compres-sion syndrome, a problem so rare there wasn't much information avail-able. One of the arteries going to my stomach was compressed by seventy percent. It could be surgically treated but not in the United States. The doctor prescribed daily medication for the GERD, but we spent a lot of time trying to figure out how to manage the celiac compression syndrome.

The stomach pain was terrible, and the doctor thought the pain was not from the GERD but from the celiac compression syndrome, but because of its rarity, she didn't know for sure. She also told me I would probably die from the syndrome—how frightening! It was so confus-ing, and the diarrhea and stomach pain continued.

On May 22nd, I finished my last year at Albuquerque Public Schools—twenty-seven years in education. I had vacillated back and forth about retiring; I was young and could still work more years, but the loss of Mom had taken its toll on me.

After her death, I became the executor of Mom's estate and that handed me a big responsibility, plus now I managed the two checking accounts for the ranch and the estate plus my own personal checking account. It was all-consuming for the sixteen months before probate ended.

With Mom gone, my brother and I managed the ranch. Bub lived in California, and since I'm only four and a half hours away, the majority of the responsibility fell on my shoulders. We had it leased, but because of a severe drought, we had to change the terms of the lease, and that took time to do—another responsibility added.

I had been around ranching all my life, but I had never been the one responsible. The learning curve was straight uphill that year; ranchers I had known my whole life suddenly became mentors to me, and I learned much from them.

In facing the added responsibility of being executor of Mom's will and co-managing the ranch, I knew it was time to retire.

I enjoyed everything about retirement, especially my freedom to go anywhere I wanted whenever I wanted. Every month I traveled to Branson to check on our two vacant houses and go out to the ranch. I loved the ability to go there as often as I wanted and needed—the monthly visits kept me connected with Mom.

On one such visit, I came across the word "leukemia" scrawled on a small scrap of paper, hidden in a desk drawer. At the sight of the word, I sobbed, but the hidden note showed me how much Mom had dwelt on that possibility.

At the end of May, Lin took me to Coronado Island near San Diego, California for my retirement present. We had a delightful time, but my stomach problems overshadowed this precious trip.

On June 27th, I turned sixty years old. Before Mom died, she had told me how she wanted to celebrate this landmark birthday. In 2012, we had thrown a big celebration surprising my brother in California. It wasn't going to be a surprise for me, because she wanted to plan it with me. Celebrating it without her was hollow at best.

I did celebrate it in Branson with Lin and Jackie and her mother, Rose. Summer, Connie's oldest daughter, came from California with Bub, and they joined us in celebrating my day. Lin bought a beautiful cake decorated with a colorful square dance couple and the Denver Broncos logo.

Two days later, we attended the annual Branson-Trinchera Reunion, as usual, and I cried in the arms of many longtime family friends. Mom had helped at this event for all the years she lived in Branson, and it was a hard day. Connie and her children came from Texas, and that helped ease the pain.

In July, Lin volunteered to be president of one of our local square dance clubs because the club was going to fold if no one took the office. The treasurer position was open, so I volunteered for that, thinking Lin would be occupied with the club, so I might as well join him.

Wow! What an experience that was! I'm a words person, not a numbers person. The job took a lot of my time, but I gradually learned the ropes. The first financial statement took me eight hours to balance, but it got easier.

My square dance commitments overflowed now because I was also the president of our dance hall, the Albuquerque Square Dance Center, and that consumed a lot of my time.

In the third weekend in August, I chaired another square and round dance event in Albuquerque, Hot August Nights. This had been a regular part of my life since 2006. It was difficult to focus and not sob every time some dear friends shared their condolences, but participating in this event helped me heal.

Before Lin and I married, I had been heavily involved with a national square dance organization for singles, Single Square Dancers USA. I was the chairperson of the annual event, Dance-A-Rama, in Albuquerque, New Mexico in 2003. I was president in 2010 and had to delay our wedding because of my commitments to the organization. This organization hosts their annual festival in a different city every year. My last official job for them was the registration chairperson for Dance-A-Rama 2013 in St. Louis, Missouri. This commitment dominated my summer and was part of the reason we didn't do much extra traveling.

Mom shared her birth date, September 24th, with Jackie Mock, our friend who helped take care of Mom in Branson. Lin and I celebrated Jackie's and Mom's birthdays in Branson with Jackie. We sobbed, missing her so.

The six-month mark was hard for me—lots of tears, sobs, and a panic attack. I spent time alone at the cemetery in Trinidad talking to Mom and Dad and sharing lunch with them. Then I went to Mom's house in Branson for time alone for me where I could cry, sob, and be with my pain. I felt the closest to her there in her home, surrounded by her personal items and all of our memories.

A major healing activity I did this first year was complete and edit a book I had written thirty years before when I participated in the National Writing Project, a professional development program for teachers. *This Tumbleweed Landed*, a poetry and prose collection about growing up in our small ranching community during the fifties and sixties, offered me the chance to focus on happier times with Mom and Dad in my childhood.

A weekly writing, exercise, and recovery meeting routine steadied me during the winter of 2014. I'd go to Jazzercise at 9:00 A.M. in Cedar Crest, New Mexico and then to my favorite coffee shop to write, edit, and revise my book until noon. Then I would attend a recovery meeting. It was on my calendar to protect the time, and I relished this time of writing and remembering happier times.

Firsts after losing someone are tough. The holidays were especially hard. Do you do the same old traditional activities or do you break with tradition and leave the country? We did the traditional.

Jackie Mock told me that a family from Trinidad parked in the driveway at Mom's house on Halloween and passed out candy—what a blessing that was. I gasped with a sob when she told me. I wasn't there to see it, but just knowing that someone was there replicating her yearly tradition helped. She so loved this holiday and prepared individual treat bags each year for the children.

To help me during this first major holiday season, Lin and I volunteered to serve Thanksgiving dinner to the homeless in Albuquerque in Mom's memory. She had always said she would like to do that, and I felt her presence that day. It was so fulfilling.

For our Thanksgiving meal, Lin and I went to the High Noon Saloon and Restaurant in Old Town Albuquerque, where we had celebrated this holiday with Mom three years earlier. I was numb—no tears, but I felt her everywhere there—it comforted my spirit.

On December 22nd, I celebrated twenty-five years of sobriety and missed Mom so much because she always recognized that day as a special day for me.

I knew Christmas would be hard! To help alleviate my grief, I made our traditional family calendar with pictures of Mom and her favorite sayings on every month. I also had pillows and pillowcases with Mom's pictures for family gifts—Mom was everywhere, which made her a part of the festivities for me.

We all enjoyed Mom's delicious pies during the holidays, so I stepped up and made them for Thanksgiving after our meal out and for Christmas, using her special German pie crust recipe.

Our plans changed drastically at the last minute. We invited Aunt Willie to join us in Branson, but she called on December 24th, saying she was sick. She also said, "Don't come to Pueblo." She couldn't come to Mom's house—it was too soon.

I took Mom's traditional chocolate-covered cherries to her neighbors across the street and exchanged gifts with Jackie and Rose. We shed lots of tears.

Lin and I went to Christmas Eve service in Des Moines, New Mexico at Mom's church and received hugs from Mom's longtime friends there. Afterwards we drove about forty-five minutes to my dad's sister's for a big family get-together. Aunt Joan shared that she regretted that she hadn't come to Albuquerque earlier to see Mom—she came the day that Mom died. She got to see her, but Mom couldn't communicate anymore.

Lin and I opened our presents Christmas morning and decided to go to Pueblo anyway. We stopped at the cemetery in Trinidad, and I got to tell Mom and Dad, "Merry Christmas." We spent the day with Aunt Willie and ate dinner at Denny's. Aunt Willie went through our family calendar month by month—each month had a favorite picture of Mom and one of her memorable sayings. She outlined the photo that was on the cover of the calendar with her index finger, tracing the familiar lines of Mom's face, and loved it.

I continued the Advent gifts for Lin and Aunt Willie this year because I couldn't stop it yet. Mom had started this tradition with me in 1988 when I went to treatment, and I added Lin and Aunt Willie in 2011 when Lin and I married. Doing it again this year helped me feel connected to Mom.

This whole holiday celebration without Mom was so heartbreaking. She was the heart and soul of my Christmas! But I survived; I didn't vomit, cry all day long, or lose my mind. Lin helped so much by hugging and holding me often.

On December 26th, Craig, Connie, and their family came over from Texas. We had a moment of serendipity on the ranch—we thought we saw a mountain lion run across in front of us. As always, we played lots of games around Mom's round table. Their being there was reminiscent of the previous year with Mom, and we often hugged each other and cried, missing her so.

Bill and Janet Berg invited us all to a big family Christmas get-together in Folsom, New Mexico on December 28th. All three of her daughters (Kirstin and her two boys, Lisa, and Meghan) and Aunt Willie were there. I gave them all photo gifts of Mom, and they loved them. Connie's family left from there to go home.

Driving home with Lin alone, I cried the whole way. I was overwhelmed with grief because Mom and I always enjoyed going home and recalling the highlights of the day.

New Year's Eve, Lin and I square danced in Albuquerque, and all evening I fought the memory of last year's sad night when Mom was so mad and so sick. As every night before this year, I slept with Mom's nightgown in my arms, but that night I needed it so much more.

When the end of January and beginning of February 2014 hit, I slid into a major depression, reliving the horror of the previous year, but I continued my normal square dance schedule and life routine.

My stomach issues had subsided some, but I had one horrible attack in early January at a dance festival in Laughlin, Nevada. I spent the first morning in bed but was able to get up and dance in the afternoon and evening. I rested off and on during the rest of the festival, not participating in the whole event, which is not like me.

I couldn't stop thinking about Mom's death and how it should have been different. I talked to Bub about it often.

On February 17th, I drove to Pueblo, Colorado and met with Mom's hematologist. Bub and I blamed him for Mom's death because he hadn't insisted she have a bone marrow biopsy, so I wanted to talk to him face-to-face. I bought a small recording device, hid it in my purse, and had it running during our conversation.

He never admitted any responsibility for the lack of the biopsy. I don't know what I thought this encounter would do—maybe that he would beg my forgiveness and admit his negligence, but he didn't. Just the brave action I took soothed my soul and put my anger to rest.

On Saturday, March 22nd, the night before the first anniversary of Mom's death, we square danced in Albuquerque but left the dance at 9:00 P.M. and drove as far as Holbrook, Arizona and spent the night. I didn't sleep well. During the evening at the dance, I kept my sorrow to myself but danced with Mom all night. She was as close as my breath throughout the night.

On March 23rd, the first anniversary of Mom's death came. Lin and I drove to Laughlin, Nevada for another square dance festival. I spent the travel time that day writing several poems—healing words and thoughts that helped take my pain away. I had such a different perspective. I pondered Mom in heaven with Dad and Jesus, and the poetry was light and whimsical.

As soon as we arrived at the casino in Laughlin, I told dance friends it was the first anniversary of Mom's death, thinking they would offer consolation and help. They mostly brushed it off like it was nothing, which shocked me. To me, it was a big deal, and I wanted them to acknowledge my pain. I spent the weekend texting a good square dance friend and my sponsor who did support me in my grief. It helped.

On our trip home from Laughlin after the festival, Sue, my sister, called and told me her husband, Fred, had stage 4 lung cancer. It had already moved to his lymph nodes and adrenal glands. I assured her that she didn't have to do this alone, and she sobbed.

This first year I followed what Mom had shown me to do when Dad died—continue living your life and grieve your way. I attended my church regularly and valued the solace I received sitting with my God, my familiar church, and my friends. Because my sobriety continued to be a major focus for me, I attended regular recovery meetings, and I stayed close to my sponsor. I threw myself into helping others one-on-one in recovery.

The hard first year ended, and I survived.

Chapter Twelve

THE SECOND YEAR FOLLOWING MOM'S DEATH MAY 2014 – DECEMBER 2015

I continued to sleep with Mom's nightgown under my pillow—her memorable fragrance gone for quite awhile, but just the sight of it comforted me.

During the year, I wrote and continued the familiar activities I loved.

Again, in May, I chaired the Duke City Singles and Doubles Square Dance Festival and continued my rich life. I gave my committee and the calling and cuing staff dishcloths I knitted—another piece of Mom because she loved to give handiwork she had made.

I continued my monthly trips to Branson to check on the two houses and the ranch. I co-managed the ranching concerns with my brother and was excited about a big change—my brother retired and moved out to his house in Branson for the summer.

We both decided to remodel the houses that we had inherited when Mom died. Bub knew what he wanted in his house: the bathroom redone totally in orange and blue for the Denver Broncos.

At first, I went wild and decided to gut the kitchen, add a dish-washer, and buy new cabinets, but when I met with the contractor in the spring and he talked about taking the kitchen cabinets out, I stepped back and reevaluated my plans. I didn't want to lose Mom's cabinets because she had handwritten notes on the inside of the doors. So I decided to go smaller: a ceiling fan in the living room, raise the shower head in the bathroom, lay cement to the back gate, and repaint the garage and trim on the house. The summer was full.

For May and June, I focused on *This Tumbleweed Landed*, revising, editing, and learning how to self-publish. I learned a lot in a short amount of time!

The boxes of my new books arrived on June 21st. Opening that box and touching my first book in print shook me to my core—a lifelong dream came true. My family surrounded me in this celebratory moment, taking pictures and congratulating me. Bub took us all to Lee's Barbecue in Trinidad for a celebration of my book.

I had no idea how far-reaching the affect it would have on my life. People bought it and told me how much they liked it. It wasn't a best-seller, but friends and family lavished many compliments on me. I had no idea that publishing that book and the aftermath would so soothe my wounded soul and validate me as an author.

Memories of Mom and Dad were a major part of that book. I had the opportunity to cherish my childhood and them. Again, writing and poetry healed my heart.

My niece, Connie, married her eighth-grade sweetheart, Craig, in Branson on June 26, 2014, the Thursday before the Branson-Trinchera reunion, so our family gathered this year for a happy celebratory time. Cheryl and Andy, my niece and nephew, brought their children, so it was a family reunion for sure.

I released my book at the reunion, and it was warmly accepted.

My family spent the days on the ranch searching out familiar spots and the evening sitting around the round table at my house, playing games, and laughing. It was a memorable time together.

I spent twenty days in Branson and the area because of all the festivities, so it was time to go home to Tijeras.

Lin and I danced locally and traveled to many of our regular out-of-town festivals but limited our travel during that summer because rebuilding our local square dance club took a lot of our time.

Bub, Lin, and I returned to Cuchara, Colorado for our Fourth of July tradition, after missing last year. We had gone there for years with Mom and knew this year would be hard. We watched the parade in the morning, then spent the day enjoying the music at the Dog Bar & Grill.

In the evening we returned to the Dog Bar and danced the night away. Bub and I had spent the Fourth of July in Cuchara with Mom since 2005 when his wife died from cancer. I saw Mom everywhere but enjoyed our time there.

In mid-August, I continued my busy life with chairing Hot August Nights.

Bub and I planned an action-packed sports weekend in Denver on August 23 – 24. On Saturday, August 23rd, we went to a Denver Broncos pre-season football game, participating in all the pre-game activities: signatures from the players as they came to the field and a picture with the Broncos cheerleaders. We had seats a couple rows from the field near the Broncos' dressing room—what a night that was! My best friend's daughter, Sonia, joined us and we had a blast. Then on Sunday Sonia met us at the Colorado Rockies baseball game to watch it. My mom was a huge Denver Broncos football fan, so Bub and I referred to her often on this trip, knowing she would have loved every minute of it.

Soon it was Mom's birthday again, but I didn't spend it in Branson, and it was a depressing day. The grief was palatable, but I didn't cry enough.

On October 26th, the Horner family received shocking news: my nephew Jason Talley had died in his early forties. What a heartbreak!

I realized that as I have aged, I have lost a lot of dear ones, and the list of dead loved ones was growing and maybe outnumbered those on this side of death. My feelings about death changed, and I toyed with many new ideas about this life and the one beyond.

I envisioned my mom and dad over there (wherever there was) with Jesus and wondered what they were doing. I thought of other loved ones I had lost and wondered. It was frightening and comforting at the same time, and it filled my thoughts.

I talked to my therapist about this newness, and she quietly questioned, "Isn't that what we're here for?" I felt confirmed and validated.

Thanksgiving was spent at the High Noon Saloon and Restaurant again, and the meal was lovely. It was hard. Last year I was numb; this year my feelings were right on the surface, ready to erupt.

After our meal, I went home and baked and froze three pies,

preparing for Christmas. Baking pies brought Mom really close to me, especially using her pie crust recipe.

After Mom passed away, I decided to publish her recipes in a cookbook for a Christmas present for my immediate family members—she had a lot of tried and tested delicious recipes. My sponsor listened to me describe this sizable project and suggested I do volumes instead of one book, so I did. I created Volume 1 of the cookbook series, which featured a fun-loving picture of Mom on the cover and had several fun photos of her in the book. I scanned in her well-worn and stained recipe cards, featuring her own handwriting, making this a unique keepsake for our family.

My family raved about it so much, I printed more copies and sold them.

I made the traditional family calendars and photo gifts.

As a retired Albuquerque Public School teacher, they hired me as a co-writer of Project Based Units for writing aimed at middle school students. In doing it, I earned an extra $2,000 and surprised Lin on December 18th with a seventy-inch flat screen TV—what a blessing to surprise this dear man.

We had planned to drive to Branson on December 23rd, but because of a snowstorm in southeastern Colorado, we delayed a day, leaving early the next morning.

Again we put up Mom's retro silver tree with purple decorations and added lights around the room. After dinner, we went to Rose's and visited with her and Jackie. I gave each of them a copy of Mom's cookbook, Volume 1, and they loved it.

We ended up not being able to see Aunt Joan this holiday because they moved their Christmas Eve celebration to Christmas day due to the snowstorm, and we had already planned to go to Pueblo to see Aunt Willie.

Christmas morning, Lin and I opened our presents, ate breakfast and left by 10:30 A.M. to go to Pueblo. Again we went by the Trinidad cemetery and wished Mom and Dad a "Merry Christmas."

As soon as we arrived, Aunt Willie opened her gifts. When she opened the cookbook and saw the picture of Mom, she grabbed her arms and said, "That gives me gooseflesh," and hugged it to her chest.

After dinner we each ate a piece of the pecan pie I baked, before going out to look at the neighborhood Christmas decorations. We decided to spend the night and when we got back, we each ate a piece of pumpkin pie. I loved being with Aunt Willie because I could feel Mom close to me there. I saw Mom so many times in different expressions of hers and it blessed my heart. Aunt Willie's sense of humor and delightful stories were a balm to my soul.

The next day we drove in the snow back to Branson. Connie, Craig, and their children arrived shortly after we did.

On December 27th, I drove Emmily, Caden, and Kaylea Raye, my two great-nieces and great-nephew, out to the ranch in the snow. The pastures sparkled pristine and white with the foot of snow from the storm. When we got to the four-mile corner, there were no tire tracks beyond the cattle guard.

Emmily challenged me to an adventure—"Come on Larada, let's make our own tracks. We can do it."—and away we went, and we got stuck.

They laid down in the snow and made snow angels and then helped me by rocking the Bronco back and forth until we got out. It was such a fun time having them there. All too soon, though, they all left that Sunday.

New Year's Eve was again spent square dancing with Lin and our friends. The square dance group celebrated the new year using Eastern time, which was two hours ahead. A group of us went to Denny's, ate, and stayed until midnight. I played "Auld Lang Syne" on my iPad, and we sang.

Chapter Thirteen

THIRD YEAR AND BEYOND: 2015 – 17

2015

January 2015, I planned to self-publish this book. I had talked to my niece Cheryl about illustrating it, but it was still too soon for me. I would start reading it and start to cry—I couldn't work on it yet.

The first two months that year hit me hard again. I dipped into depression again, remembering Mom's last three months.

Each morning, I did my quiet time, writing and reading with my cat, Jesse, close to me. I loved my rich, full life—writing, dancing, traveling, visiting Branson monthly, recovery meetings and time with my sponsor and sponsees, and all the volunteer activities I did for square dancing.

But deep inside, I ached. The pain always resided just below the surface but seemed to be more raw and prevalent January through March.

On January 10th, my brother-in-law, Fred Buhr, died—another death for the Horner family of someone taken too soon by cancer.

The second anniversary of Mom's death drew near. On March 21st, we square danced in Albuquerque. I kept my sorrow to myself but danced with Mom all night, drawing solace from the habit that dated clear back to my childhood and dancing every Saturday night with my family. We left the dance early and drove as far as Gallup, New Mexico and spent the night. I didn't sleep well.

On Sunday, we headed for the square and round dance festival in Laughlin, Nevada and again I faced the anniversary of Mom's death at this square dance event. After my friends' behavior the previous year concerning Mom's death, I had no expectations about how I would be treated, so I handled it much easier.

I couldn't believe it had been two years—at times it seemed like the time flew by, but at other times, it seemed to crawl. How had I survived two years without Mom? I wondered about it all day—it had been easier than the year before but still so profoundly difficult. Many people think you should be over a death within six months to a year, and here it was two years later, and I still felt raw and vulnerable about my loss.

Again I chaired Duke City Singles and Doubles Spring Fling the first weekend of May.

I continued to work on this grief book, but it was too soon and too fresh. When I began to read it, my heart hurt too much, so I put it aside.

Bub decided to stay longer in Colorado, so I had him to help with the ranch from May to September. We both did more renovations on our two houses, filling the summer.

I didn't attend the Branson-Trinchera Reunion because Lin and I went to the National Square Dance Convention in Springfield, Massachusetts. My birthday occurred while we were there, and I felt so alone so far away from home and family. So I played a voicemail of Mom's birthday greetings I had kept from 2012, and I cried and cried. She'd always made my birthdays so special, and I missed her so.

We did our traditional Fourth of July celebration at the Dog Bar and Grill in Cuchara and danced the evening away as usual.

Bub and I bought a Kawasaki Mule, a side-by-side to ride around the ranch.

The ranch received an unusual amount of rain, so the reservoirs were full and the grass measured the tallest it had been in years.

Bub and I continued our renovations on the houses: he took up the sixty-year-old carpet and had the hardwood floors refinished to a beautiful shine. We then bought Native American rugs from Chimayo, New Mexico for his living room and dining room.

Mom had always wanted to put in new windows throughout, but she didn't get to achieve that dream. I decided it was time to do it—to honor Mom's wishes. I also put up a door to close off the unfinished basement for a couple reasons: it helped in heating the house, and I'd be able to bring my cat, Jesse, with me to Branson without worrying about keeping him off of the back porch.

At the end of July, we had a mini-family gathering in Branson. Andy brought his two daughters, AnnDeeClaire and Daisylinn, from California, and Connie and her three children came from Texas. We filled our days with visits to the ranch and really enjoyed riding around on the Mule. Everyone enjoyed shooting guns and target practicing. In the evenings, we played games.

One evening after a thunderstorm, I reminisced about the electricity going out when I was a child and the fun we had using the kerosene lamps for lighting, so we turned off the lights and used the kerosene lamps. The children enjoyed a step back into the past.

After everyone left, I had a weepy morning, missing Mom and being alone after having so many there. Mom loved it when everyone came to visit but hated it when everyone left. I usually scheduled my departure a day or so to ease her transition. Now I knew how she felt.

In August, again I chaired the square and round dance festival in Albuquerque, Hot August Nights.

I spent Mom's birthday in Branson with Bub and Jackie, but the pain had subsided and her absence was noted but not the focus.

Another story of mine had laid dormant for thirty-five years —*When Will Papa Get Home?*, a historical fiction closely connected to Dad. It's based on a blue marble I found at my favorite homestead one day when we were out exploring. Dad and Granddad had repeatedly retold the story of Philly, the owner of that homestead. He was thrown in jail for being a cow thief. My granddad bought that piece of land from the local DA when Philly was in jail.

We were getting ready to leave the homestead and I looked down. Between the front step and door lay a blue marble. I asked Dad whose it was and he had no idea.

"Probably arrowhead hunters who were out here looking around."

His answer wasn't sufficient for me. That marble and its rightful owner rolled around in my head, and most of the story came to me years ago, but now I filled in the gaps. I researched the historical aspects of the story and again writing healed me.

I beefed up the book with research, adding ten thousand words to the manuscript, and self-published it in November. Again people raved about it, and once more I celebrated my family and our ranch in the written word.

More healing and time had eased my pain and I no longer felt the looming dread for the holidays that I'd felt before.

I went alone to Branson the three days before Thanksgiving, and it was bittersweet. On the way back to Tijeras, I met my friend Scott Warner for lunch and then I went to the cemetery and put out Christmas flowers on Mom's and Dad's graves. Being there the day before Thanksgiving was heart-wrenching and wonderful at the same time.

Thanksgiving came, and Lin and I returned to the High Noon Saloon and Restaurant for dinner. Softly, Mom skirted our dinner—I felt her presence but not as strong as the previous years.

I continued the cookbook series that Christmas. I sold Volume 2 with my other books.

A major snowstorm hit southeastern Colorado, so the regular holiday plans were changed. We went to Mom's church for Christmas Eve service. Normally we scurried up to Aunt Joan's on Christmas Eve, but because of the storm, she moved her celebration to Christmas Day. She had thirty-three people seated for dinner. It was quite a family celebration.

On December 26th, we went to Pueblo to be with Aunt Willie, my cousins, Janet and Bill Berg, and their oldest daughter, Kirstin, and her fiancé, Dane, and her two boys. It was nice, but Lin and I were used to having Aunt Willie to ourselves, so it wasn't as personal as the previous years. We had to leave late afternoon to get back to Branson, where Connie and her family would join us again like last year. We ended up traveling the whole way home in a snowstorm again. On the way, we found out that Connie's son, Caden, was sick and so they had to cancel their visit to us. I missed our usual full house of kids, laughter, and activity. Connie's family had become a major part of my Christmas celebration after Mom's death.

This was a stressful Christmas season with sickness and the snowstorm.

We drove home on New Year's Eve and faced a snow-covered driveway. After helping Lin shovel the drive, I showered and noticed red lines that itched on the tops of my feet. I had a break out of contact dermatitis, so we celebrated New Year's Eve sitting on the love seat with my feet propped up watching TV together. I had Mom on my mind all night. It was hard not to remember the sadness of our last New Year's Eve together.

❄

2016

My busy life kept me going—Mom always enjoyed hearing about my different interests and commitments. Following her advice, I continued my normal life, and she was the wisp of memory every morning when I got up and saw her nightgown under my pillow and when I asked her to join me for my day in my quiet time. Truly time had healed the deep wound in my heart.

The third anniversary of Mom's death passed. There was no dance to attend because of the day of the week it occurred. I had to face the day without any distractions, and I did, but it wasn't easy. Three years —so hard to imagine life without her for that long.

On April 18, 2016, my brother-in-law, Ron Talley, died in Colorado Springs. The losses continued.

Again, I chaired Duke City Singles and Doubles Spring Fling, but that year it was the last weekend in April instead of the first of May.

During the year, I had an energizing focus—my books. I attended several events to sell them, and my sales pitch became perfected: "These books are about my family. The cookbook collection is full of my mom's delicious recipes. This book is about my dad and how my grandfather put our ranch together in southeastern Colorado during the depression when many ranchers were losing theirs. This book is about my experience in our small ranching community and ranch during the fifties and sixties. And this one is a historical fiction set on our ranch."

had put together a collection of books that celebrated my mom
dad and our life together, and every time I retold that sales pitch, I
ood a little taller and it gladdened my heart.

Again, I had plans to publish this grief book in June 2016, but it
didn't happen. The poetry was written for the most part, but the book's
organization baffled me. At first, it was to be just about Mom's death,
then I realized that I needed to add the story of Dad's death to give a
complete picture of my universal losses.

After Mom's death, a square dance friend asked me if I felt like an
orphan. Yes, I am an adult orphan. My parents had been intimately
involved in my life, so that idea really explained the deep loss I felt and
I wanted it to be a part of this book.

But I still had them with me, in my heart, and around me in the
people I love.

For my birthday that year, Lin, Bub, and I went to Pueblo and cele-
brated it with Aunt Willie—she so appreciated it and again it felt like
time with Mom.

Bub enjoyed the last summer in Colorado so much that he came
earlier in May and stayed until the first part of November. The renova-
tions continued on the two houses in Branson. Bub remodeled his back
porch, painting the walls bright orange and the trim blue for the Denver
Broncos. I had a new front porch put on my house.

In December 2008, I had bought a townhouse when my third
husband and I divorced. Mom spent a lot of time there with me, so that
place was full of our memories. I had kept it after Lin and I married
because Mom had told me once that she would feel safe living there.
I'd planned for it to be a place for her live out her life, close to me, but
that didn't work out. I sold it in August 2016. My last day there was a
teary, sad one, remembering all the fun Mom and I had there. It ended
an era for us.

In mid-September, Lin, Bub, and I returned to Pueblo to celebrate
Lin's birthday with Aunt Willie.

Our Thanksgiving tradition continued: a late lunch at the High
Noon Saloon and Restaurant in Old Town Albuquerque. Lin and I
had a precious time. Again, a wisp of Mom appeared slightly with
the coriander soup she loved. She lived on in my memory of her
there.

Christmas came with me celebrating Mom in the next volume of my cookbook series, *From Grannie's Kitchen*, and I continued the Christmas tradition of our family calendar and gifts with family photos on them.

We spent Christmas Eve in Branson and went to Pueblo on Christmas Day to be with Aunt Willie.

Lin and I had another strange New Year's Eve. The year before we'd stayed home on New Year's Eve because of my feet; this year Lin was sick, so I had a lonely time seated on our love seat, with Lin upstairs in bed. I tried to find a New Year's Eve show to watch and enjoy but wasn't too successful. I didn't know all these new actors and actresses—I missed Dick Clark. Mom's sad, haunting presence from 2012 had slipped away, though, and I remembered more joyful New Year's Eves with her.

❄

2017

Again, I filled my life with promoting my three books and my cookbook series and attended many promotional events.

My passions continued to be the focus of my life: writing, traveling, dancing, going to Branson monthly, and doing all the volunteer work I do for square dancing. I love my full, rich retired life.

The fourth anniversary of Mom's death just passed. I sat next to my cat, Jesse, like so many other mornings, and I cried. I honored the day, called my brother, and we talked about our loss. I reflected all day about the never-ending loss of my mom, but I also celebrated who she was in my life—grateful for the many years we shared.

In mid-April, I enjoyed five days in Branson and spent one day revising the sections of this book about Mom and her decline. It was a day of tears and memories. I sobbed as I haven't in a couple years, and I knew in my core that it was a cleansing at a deeper level. Seeing it from the distance of four years added a new clarity.

Today, after I finish the final revision of this book, I will be attending our annual square dance festival: the Duke City Singles and Doubles Spring Fling. This week has been filled to overflowing with preparation for that event and revisions for this book.

Looking back to four years ago and where I was with my unbearable pain, today I rejoice in where I am in my process of completing this book and honoring the loss of my parents and my pain. My heart is singing!

After experiencing Mom's death, I did not run away physically or emotionally but stood tall and solid. I realized a strong truth about myself. I am who I always wanted to be: strong in crisis, dependable, loyal, loving, and supportive. The little girl who lives within me wasn't sure that I could do it, but I did—and I will!

I faced grief head-on and am convinced that I have figured it out for now—I truly grew up in the process, becoming the woman I always wanted to be.

APPENDIX A

It's a God Thing!

I knew without a doubt that my God was beside me and in the midst of this whole ordeal of losing Mom. I believe that my life is a spiritual experience, and as a regular part of my day, I am on the watch for God actively participating in my life. I carefully search for those telling moments when God quietly yet profoundly appears in an event or an experience and shouts to my soul, "I am here. I am in control. I love you!"

Here's a list of the numerous God incidents that occurred during those three months from Mom getting sick and dying:

- I was sober and present and able to be of service to my mom.
- Bub, Lin, and I worked as a team to support Mom—long distance while Bub was still in California and then close-knit once he came to New Mexico.
- Lin supported us in another way: he stepped back and let Bub and I do our work together and supported me in the background.
- Karen White, my supervisor at Albuquerque Public schools, released me often to work at the hospital or at home during

those three crazy months. She never questioned my work ethic and supported me completely. My colleagues did, too, and their support was invaluable.

- I took a silver iced tea spoon of Lin's to the hospital so Mom could scoop ice cream out of a glass. Ice cream was one item she could eat, and one of the nurses said it provided a lot of the nutrients she needed. Accidentally, the spoon went off to the gigantic cafeteria to be washed with all the other dishes. I talked to the nurse about its disappearance and wondered if we could get it back. She shook her head, doubting if we would ever see it again. It took several days, but we got it back! Not a surprise at all.

- Bub and Cheryl, his youngest daughter, came the first part of March. It was Cheryl who picked up on Mom having trouble swallowing, which became a big issue later. Connie, Bub's oldest daughter, was with us the day Mom passed away. Andy, Bub's son, came immediately after Mom died. He was with us to help with funeral arrangements. He also went to Colorado Springs with me to meet with our estate lawyer. Bub was sick and couldn't go. The timing for these three helping was perfect, but no one planned it.

- When Mom was diagnosed with myelofibrosis, the hospital chaplain prayed with her, leading her through a visualization with Jesus. I watched her face as she processed the images. She so believed in the positive views of life, death, and Jesus the chaplain shared. Her spirit calmed down after that.

- At the hospital where Mom received such wonderful care, Reese was the GM unit nurse who looked after Mom so carefully. She admired Bub's and my dedication to Mom and how we worked together. She said so many elderly people come into the hospital with no family to assist them. She complimented us often.

- A couple weeks before Mom passed, she was at a skilled nursing facility, but they couldn't provide the care she needed. I felt that the hospice at one particular hospital would be the panacea for Mom because my good friend,

Kathi Raver, had died there, but my God had a different plan. Mom went back to the hospital she had just been released from because she couldn't eat and the hospice I wanted her to go into couldn't deal with that problem. Mom received exceptional care at the hospital again and was transferred to their in-hospital hospice for three hours before she passed away, and the transition was smooth and easy.

- Ten days before Mom died, she faced a scary ambulance ride from the skilled nursing facility back to the hospital. The two EMTs let me ride in the back with her to hold her hand and calm her down. It had been a grueling, long wait for the ambulance because the nausea had returned with a vengeance, and she was upset about having to go back to the hospital.

- The last week of Mom's life was hectic. I didn't trust the hospital with what we hoped would be a (very expensive) miracle drug. I was told that I needed to meet with their pharmacist about the distribution of the expensive drug. It was late afternoon. I had sat down to catch my breath after a grueling day at the hospital. Someone slid into the seat beside me, and I didn't look up. When I finally turned, I didn't recognize her at first. She whispered, "You were my eighth grade English teacher in Raton." It was Jenny Bacca Mills, the pharmacist I needed to talk to and an old student of mine. With everything going on that day, this felt ordained. I cried and cried. She hugged me as we talked, and I felt God had given her to me at this crucial time.

- While Mom was in the hospital, Rhonda Sandoval, my teaching teammate and longtime friend, visited twice and brightened Mom up both times. One time she brought a colorful plant; another time she brought a delicious homemade pie. Her presence soothed my stress, and her thoughtful questions and considerations helped me process so much of the massive information I was juggling.

- Dr. Wilson was Mom's last rotation doctor at the hospital. The hospital rotated her doctor each week, and we were lucky to have Dr. Wilson at the end. She was so gentle and soft-spoken but strong. She was the best one to be assigned when Mom passed.

- On the day Mom died, Dr. Wilson transferred Mom over to the in-hospital hospice instead of transferring her to another outside facility where she would have had to endure another ambulance ride. God is good!

- The young, empathetic oncologist, who told me the truth about Jakafi, comforted us on Mom's last day. She gave me great advice before I could even ask her for it: "If this was my Grandma, I would admit her to hospice and love her until she goes."

- Mom was surrounded all day by family who loved her on the day she died.

- Mom died on a Saturday evening—ready to dance the evening away in heaven with Dad like so many other Saturdays in their life together.

- Pam Bernal (Wendelin) and her husband, John, were the ambulance drivers who took Mom from Albuquerque, New Mexico to Trinidad, Colorado to the mortuary. Pam had been a dear friend of Mom's for years, and I knew Mom was in good hands.

- I asked Bub to join Lisa and me to pick out the outfit Mom would be buried in instead of assuming that because he's a man he wouldn't be interested. It was important that he was a part of that decision, and we had a memorable day.

- Lisa's humor and positive, loving spirit relieved an unbearable day as we picked out Mom's burial outfit. She loved her "Auntie Elva" so much and that deep care permeated our time together.

- Sitting at the round table in Branson with Bub and Andy, creating Mom's memorial service, I remembered from out of the blue Mom saying my whole life, "I want 'Stardust' played at my funeral."

- Searching in her desk, paperwork, and Bible for some directions for her funeral, I found a sheet of paper that identified three favorite Bible verses she wanted read at her funeral: Psalms 150:4, II Timothy 3:16, and Ecclesiastes 3:1-8.

- So many people came from far away for Mom's service. Those who couldn't come sent cards. What dear, supportive friends!
- My great-nieces and -nephews hunted Easter eggs that Easter in Mom's yard and I knew that Mom and Dad were enjoying the sight from heaven.
- Not our first choice, Mom's funeral was set for April 1st due to another service that same weekend for a dear friend of Mom's, Alice. The decision to push the date out made it a longer wait, but our small, tight-knit ranching communities in southeastern Colorado are that important. Bub and I were then able to attend Alice's funeral and support their family in their time of need, and one of Alice's sons came to Mom's and supported us.
- Mom's memorial service being on April Fools' Day was almost fitting. She loved to pull practical jokes on any unsuspecting loved one. It also was Helen Waldroup's birthday, her best friend.

APPENDIX B

Activities I Did

How did I deal with the grief? What did I actually do? Here is a list of the activities I did after Mom died. Notice I focused on grief but mostly the activities were a part of my normal life.

- Planned Mom's service with my brother, Bub, and his son, Andy. I honored her wishes at her service. We played music to honor her, both before and during the service, and had crowd participation during the eulogy.
- Outlined Mom's lips the day of her funeral because the funeral director didn't get them right. I knew deeply that the physical shell laying in the coffin wasn't my mom; her captivating spirit was my mom.
- Enjoyed my family when we were together for Mom's memorial service. We celebrated life during Easter. We collaborated on her eulogy, using the poem read at her seventy-fifth birthday party as the basis.
- Went to a George Strait concert in Albuquerque, New Mexico with my husband and brother the Friday after Mom's service. We planned this before Mom died. Music had been a major part of our life, so it seemed fitting.

- Slept with Mom's last nightgown in my arms for weeks, the scent of her surrounding me. After the scent faded away, I moved it under my pillow and it's still there today.
- Found a pair of my panties in Mom's dresser drawer and realized that she had tucked them away one time I was home after she had done my laundry. I gasped as the tears came—I knew she loved me and cherished our limited time together, but this little action touched me deeply.
- Continued monthly massage appointments that were a major part of my self-care routine. My massage therapist is my ex-mother-in-law, and she knew and loved my mom. We spent a lot of our time reminiscing about Mom before and after my appointments.
- Did my morning quiet time that I have done for years. My cat, Jesse, joined me each morning and snuggled close to me. This was our routine:
- Wrote my three "Morning Pages" in my journal.
- Asked Mom to join me daily. A friend at a meeting suggested this.
- Read my meditation books daily. Added a daily meditation book about grief.
- Had a daily appointment to cry. It was a suggestion from the grief counselor from the hospice Grief Support Group and it helped so much.
- Brushed and stroked Jesse.
- Attended my church regularly, cried openly, and asked for prayers.
- Attended the Jewish Grief Support Group immediately.
- Attended the hospice Grief Support Group until I felt I didn't need it.
- Dealt with my anger about my loss. When I was alone in Branson, Colorado, I screamed and beat the bed. I cried and yelled at my God for taking my mom way too soon.
- Shared my pain with people who loved Mom. Our shared memories helped ease the loss.
- Continued sand play therapy with my therapist, Susan

Macnofsky, and read to her my poetry I wrote about my grief.

- Went to Jazzercise and worked out my anger and pain.
- Continued my recovery work—I attended regular meetings and met with my sponsor and my sponsees.
- Said a silent prayer and cried the third Saturday of each month at the exact time Mom died. I did this for several months.
- Wrote lots of poetry when the grief overwhelmed me.
- Danced as often as I possibly could.
- Talked and talked and talked to Bub, Lin, and anyone who would listen.
- Enjoyed looking at pictures of Mom—organized pictures I had of her at all ages on my computer. Not doing a PowerPoint presentation at her service was sad to me because I am a PowerPoint specialist and had done presentations for family and friend's memorial services, so I organized a bunch of her pictures for myself.
- Wrote, wrote, and wrote.
- Regularly went to the cemetery in Trinidad, Colorado and had lunch with Dad and Mom and cried. Wrote poetry and talked to them while eating. It was a regular date when I was in the Trinidad area.
- Didn't clear out Mom's personal belongings immediately. Three years later and I have only gotten rid of most of Mom's clothes and personal items. (We are keeping her house as a second house, so there was no need to get rid of furniture and big items.)
- Knitted more than thirty-five dishcloths—the rhythmic, simple repetition soothed me. I could escape the pain by doing something repetitive with my hands and the pattern was so simple, I didn't have to think—it was a form of meditation for sure. Also my mom was a passionate handiworker—she sewed, crocheted, and did embroidery. As I knitted, I saw her crooked, arthritic hands moving effortlessly in my hands, and I felt connected to her.
- Entered some of Mom's genealogy information into a

computer program. Her black genealogy book was her prized possession, so I felt connected to her working with it.

- Handled the load of being executor of her will—that demanding activity kept me centered in my loss and busy —very busy!
- Managed the two bank accounts for the estate and the ranch.
- Co-managed the ranch with Bub.
- Changed my attitude about grief—as I wrote my "Morning Pages" in my journal and my poetry, I saw that it lessened the pain.
- Decorated Dad's and Mom's graves on each Memorial Day since Mom passed. Their generation traditionally continued this activity. Since Mom died, I have decorated all of the family graves in the Trinidad cemetery and enjoyed the reminiscing.
- Changed the flowers on their graves for the different seasons. Because I enjoy visiting their graves, this has been fairly easy to keep up.
- Carried through with chairperson's responsibility six weeks after my mom died for a square and round dance festival. Gave solar flowers as gifts to the staff of the festival in memory of Mom, who loved those dancing flowers.
- Experienced my first Christmas without Mom. I made Mom the center of our Christmas, giving the family presents I'd made with Mom's pictures on them. We celebrated Mom that first Christmas—she was everywhere, especially there for me in the many hours of preparation of each of these projects.
- Visited our family home in Branson, Colorado, where I felt closest to Mom, monthly.
- Hid small, insignificant possessions of Mom's away for several months at our house because I couldn't bear to throw them away immediately. One day I found her bottom wipes in our downstair's bathroom and threw them away without thinking. It was time. This helped me start letting go and getting rid of Mom's stuff.

- Read a variety of grief books to nurture my soul. See Appendix C. Read grief booklets that Macky Gibbs Pitt, a lifelong friend and minister now, sent me in the first year.
- Had Mom's favorite t-shirts and blouses made into two quilts for my brother and me to commemorate her and keep her present with us! That quilt dons my bed in Branson.
- Went to Pueblo, Colorado October 2013 and brought Aunt Willie back to the cemetery in Trinidad to put an angel plaque on Mom's grave and then celebrated our wedding anniversary with her in Pueblo. It was a hard, blessed day.
- Collected Mom's look-alike Christmas outfits and sent them to Mary Jo, a friend who had lost everything she owned in the Little Bear Fire in Ruidoso, New Mexico, moved to Virginia, and was Mom's size. I couldn't bear giving those precious outfits to Goodwill and possibly see them here in the Albuquerque area. I wanted to know where they were going to be.
- Collected her coats the winter of 2013 and gave them to my church to give to homeless people.
- Served Thanksgiving dinner with Lin to the homeless in Albuquerque in Mom's memory in 2013.
- Celebrated Christmas 2013 at my cousin Janet's house the day after Christmas with Aunt Willie, Bill, Janet, and their three daughters and two grandsons. They helped me deal with that first year without Mom.
- Spent the first anniversary morning of Mom's death writing poetry as we drove to Laughlin, Nevada for a square dance event. Years before, Mom had attended a festival there with my ex-husband and me, so I felt her presence there.
- Spent the second anniversary going to the same square dance event in Laughlin, Nevada. Dancing heals my heart.
- Accomplished a big dream—no, seven big dreams!
- Published *This Tumbleweed Landed*, June 2014—a poetry and prose collection I had written over thirty years ago about growing up in our small ranching community during the fifties and sixties.
- Published *From Grannie's Kitchen, Volume 1 – Pies, Cakes*

and Candy, Christmas 2014—the first cookbook of Mom's recipes. I created it as a Christmas present for our family that first Christmas without Mom. She was center stage for Christmas, which helped me deal with her absence.

- Reprinted *Let Me Tell You a Story*, October 2015 (Originally printed for my dad's seventy-fifth birthday, 1993)—Mom recorded Dad telling the story of how Granddad Horner put our family ranch together during the depression, then she transcribed it and I transferred it to a computer. Dad and I edited the document together, then Mom and I had it professionally printed for his seventy-fifth birthday present and also printed copies for family members.

- Published *When Will Papa Get Home?*, November 2015—a historical fiction I wrote thirty-five years ago based on a story I had heard repeatedly growing up about a homestead on our ranch. Mom and Dad are in the story.

- Published *From Grannie's Kitchen, Volume 2 – Beverages, Bread, Cookies, Meats, Vegetables, Misc. & Records of a Rancher's Wife*, Christmas 2015—the second cookbook of Mom's recipes. This provided another Christmas for me to enjoy Mom's presence in a profound way.

- Published *From Grannie's Kitchen, Volume 3 – Casseroles, Mexican Dishes, Relish, Sandwiches, Salads & Desserts*, Christmas 2016—the last volume of the cookbook series of Mom's recipes. It felt right to end this series, but it was sad at the same time.

- Published *A Time to Grow Up: A Daughter's Grief Memoir*, June 2017— this book chronicles my journey through my grief process and helped me come to grips with a major awareness in my life—I grew up to be the woman I always wanted to be!

APPENDIX C

Books that were helpful to me:

Being Mortal, Atul Gawande, Henry Holt & Co., 2014

A Year to Live, How to Live This Year As If It Were Your Last, Stephen Levine, Three Rivers Press, 2009

Good Grief, Granger E. Westberg, Fortress Press, 2011

Healing After Loss: Daily Meditations for Working Through Grief, Martha Whitmore Hickman, William Morrow Paperbacks, 1994

His Last Steps, Earnie Larsen, Hazelden Foundation, 2012

On Death & Dying, Elizabeth Kubler-Ross, Scribner, Reprint Edition 2011

Stephen Series

A Time to Grieve, Book One, Kenneth C. Haugk, Stephen Ministries, 2004

Experiencing Grief, Book Two, Kenneth C. Haugk, Stephen Ministries, 2004

Finding Hope and Healing, Book Three, Kenneth C. Haugk, Stephen Ministries, 2004

Rebuilding and Remembering, Book Four, Kenneth C. Haugk, Stephen Ministries, 2004

Helpful web sites:

David Kessler's web site—worked with Elisabeth Kubler-Ross &
Louise Hay
http://grief.com

Griefshare—grief support groups all over the USA
https://www.griefshare.com

The Grief Toolbox—Articles, artworks, groups and books
http://thegrieftoolbox.com

GriefNet—On-line grief support and books
https://www.griefnet.org

American Hospice Foundation
https://americanhospice.org

Elisabeth Kubler-Ross Foundation
http://www.ekrfoundation.org

APPENDIX D

Workbook

Healing from grief requires active participation if you want to get past the pain and the loss to the other side—to thrive more than just survive. Here are a few questions and activities to get the juices flowing after reading this book.

1. List the key people you have lost in your life and write out a short description of your relationship beside the name of each person. How did that loss affect you? How old were you? How did you handle your grief at the time? What did you learn about your grief process?

2. How do you feel about grief after reading this book? What do you know about grief? Where could you find more information about grief?

3. If applicable: how did your mother grieve the loss of her parents? How did your father grieve the loss of his parents? Which one are you more like? Write down three take-aways you learned from your parents about how to grieve.

ANSWER QUESTIONS IN SPACE PROVIDED BELOW.

4. What resources do you have available when you lose a loved one? (Example: Friends, church, social support group, etc.) Write down names, phone numbers, and email addresses to have available.

5. Be diligent about the following areas of your life because grief affects the whole person. Identify one activity you can do to take care of yourself in each of these areas:

Physical —
Emotional —
Spiritual —

6. Buy a journal and/or adult coloring book and colored pencils/crayons and draw your feelings. Use this as a journal and dedicate time often to color and then describe the drawing.

8. Create a sacred time and place every day to cry. Mark it on your calendar: when and where, and be dedicated about keeping that time.

9. Get involved in a grief support group in your area. Examples: Grief-Share, hospice, religious groups, yoga, etc.

10. Look at Appendix A and start a "God Things" list for what you are going through right now. Be sure not to leave out what seems small and insignificant.

ANSWER QUESTIONS IN SPACE PROVIDED BELOW.

11. Look at Appendix B and identify the normal activities you do that soothe your soul and then add activities to support your grief process.

12. Look at Appendix C and select one book to add to your library and read it. Search the topic "grief" online and add any titles below that appeal to you.

13. On the first anniversary of your loved one's death, plan ahead to be prepared and make it a special day for you.

ABOUT THE AUTHOR

In addition to *A Time to Grow Up*, Larada Horner-Miller is the author of *This Tumbleweed Landed* and *When Will Papa Get Home?* Both were finalists for the 2016 New Mexico–Arizona Book Awards.

Horner-Miller received a bachelor's degree in English, with a minor in Spanish, and a master's degree in education, with a specialty in integrating technology in the classroom. She spent thirteen years as a beautician and twenty-seven years as an educator. She now comanages her family ranch with her brother.

Horner-Miller lives in Tijeras, New Mexico, with her husband, Lin, and cat, Jesse.

I would love to hear from you!
www.larada.wix.com/author
larada@earthlink.net

ALSO BY LARADA HORNER-MILLER

This Tumbleweed Landed

When Will Papa Get Home?

Let Me Tell You a Story

From Grannie's Kitchen Cookbook Series:

- *Pies, Cakes & Christmas Candy, Volume 1*
- *Beverages, Cookies, Meats, Vegetables, Mis. & Records of a Rancher;'s Wife, Volume 2*
- *Casseroles, Mexican Dishes, Relish, Sandwiches, Salads & Desserts, Volume 3*

FUTURE PROJECTS

- *Marshall Flippo* - Biography of a legendary square dance caller
- *Eyewitness to Life* - Fiction
- *This Tumbleweed Landed Volume Two* - More poetry and prose

ABOUT THE ILLUSTRATOR

Cheryl Horner-Christensen is an artist at heart and a cake decorator. She graduated with a Bachelors Degree in Liberal Studies and a concentration in Literature and Communication from San Francisco State University.

For the last 7 years she has been building her own cake decorating business, Cheryl's Custom Creations, to express her artistic cravings.

This is Cheryl's first opportunity to have her illustrations published and has more projects lined up for future publication.

Cheryl resides in Clearlake Oaks, CA with her husband and two sons.

Contact Cheryl for more information:
cheryltggr@gmail.com

f

EXCERPT FROM MY NEW BOOK, "EYE WITNESS TO LIFE"

Release date: 2019.

The ATM machine would not take her money. A cold winter breezed blew her unbuttoned coat apart and she grabbed at the neck of her wayward coat to keep the cold out. I saw that she wore an worn apron under her coat. Her blonde strands blew aimlessly around her face, and her uncovered hands looked cold.

What was she doing?

Another work day had ended, and I needed to get home to cook dinner for my husband and me. I had to stay at school for a teacher meeting and a parent conference that took longer than I expected. I had papers to grade after dinner.

On the way home, I stopped by my sister, Susie's, house to pick up a new outfit that she had bought for me at a great price online on Lulily's. When I got there, I realized I didn't have any cash, so I ran over to the ATM at the Smith's store, close to her house.

The bewildered woman tried again, looking at the president's face on the bill and trying to decide if she had it pointing in the right direction. Then she tried again, growing more desperate with each attempt to insert it in the right position so the ATM would accept the bill.

An anxious crowd continued to gather respectfully behind her, giving her the space they seemed to think she needed. The blustery winter day added to the lengthy wait. Someone in the silent crowd recognized her and called her husband. They continued to wait, almost reverent in the space they gave her.

She continued her effort; the crowd seemed paralyzed by her senseless behavior. No one went forward to help her. I felt as powerless as everyone else. I searched theirs face and I saw empathy. I stamped my numb feet and patted my gloved hands. Others did the same.

Within a few minutes his car screeched to a halt behind the gathering. He pushed his way through the crowd and rushed to her side.

"Laura, come home with me."

His voice broke her out of the trance she was in, and she evaluated the situation. Here she was at an ATM machine trying to put money back into it--in the card slot. For the first time since the crowd had formed, she realized that what she was doing wouldn't work. She started sobbing.

His gentle words caressed her as much as his arms did. He moved her to his Chevy Tahoe, and they drove away. Her vacant stare out the passenger window caught my eyes, as I waited in the group. She seemed so small and frail—so lost.

Who was this lady who had a world so turned upside down she was trying to put money back in an ATM machine? What support her husband showed for her.

The group left waiting did the business at hand. We were silent for awhile, in honor of this woman's pain and confusion. Someone finally broke the silence with a simple question that all our hearts echoed, "What happened to her to put her into such a confused state?"

We did not judge her in this question--only true concern. For me, I identified with her. My world had been a little shaky lately, and the fear of dropping off the deep end hung over me like a black death shroud. Her vacant eyes haunted me!

I waited my turn. Silence enveloped this group who had witnessed this strange situation. When my time came, I simply stepped up to the machine, put my debit card into the slot where she had tried so hard to jam a $20 bill in and got the money I needed. This was a simple task I did often, but this incident was etched in memory forever.

I ran by Susie's house real fast, gave her the money and didn't say anything about the ATM experience because I was so late getting home. I thanked her for the awesome outfit she bought me. She often called me about a dress or outfit she wanted me to buy online. I didn't do much shopping online, but she did and I often benefited from her frugal shopping. I told her as I ran out the door that I would call her tomorrow with a really strange occurrence.

I pondered the group question asked all the way home, not aware of the traffic or scenery I drove through. I traveled the familiar route that I drove every day after work.

I turned on our street, back in my familiar neighborhood. I breathed a sigh of relief. As I pulled up into the driveway and clicked the garage door open, I shuttered. I watched the metallic door go up in its slow methodical track as it did every day—something I have taken for granted for years. I pulled up into the garage and dreaded going inside.

I needed to share what had happened with my husband but wondered how I could put into words what had just happened to me.

George, my husband greeted me in his usual distant manner from behind his wall of attachment to the TV. His eyes never left the screen and I knew better than talking now because his attention was locked onto whatever was there. I noticed it so differently today after witnessing her husband's nurturing words and manner.

Would George act accordingly if he found me in a incoherent stupor? Would he rescue me from the ATM machine and what appeared to be sheer stupidity, but everyone present knew it was not?

That evening happened like so many others have. After fixing dinner with the TV blaring, we ate our meal with minimal amount of conversation about nothing. George doesn't even ask about my day anymore even though I religiously ask him about his and listen to him drone on and on.

I did the dishes; he watched TV. I joined him watching his favorite TV shows for the evening for awhile.

Before it got too late, I went to my office and checked email. I did the five things I had to get done tonight to prepare for tomorrow's classroom. You see, I'm a teacher.

I like my home office. I have it decorated in a warm Southwest decor and photos from trips I've taken to Central and South America. It is my refuge in this home that has been a hostile environment for me for most of our marriage.

www.ingramcontent.com/pod-product-compliance
Lightning Source LLC
Chambersburg PA
CBHW031230090426
42742CB00007B/136